Customer
Integration

Customer Integration

The Quality Function Deployment (QFD) Leader's Guide for Decision Making

Doug Daetz, Bill Barnard, and Rick Norman

John Wiley & Sons, Inc.
New York • Chichester • Brisbane • Toronto • Singapore

Contents

Part II
Implementation Context and Guidance for the Middle and Program/Project Manager

Part III
The Project-Level Practitioner

Appendices

List of Tables and Figures

Tables

Figures

Read Me First

The purpose of this book is to introduce and define a robust, practical, integrated, and proven process called "Customer-Integrated Decision-Making (CIDM)." It is a structured process incorporating customer research and solution development that builds on Quality Function Deployment (QFD). CIDM/QFD has been proven by the authors in over one hundred implementations over the last seven years to over fifty companies worldwide. The CIDM methodology is an integrated approach that companies can use to achieve success in a timely manner by developing the right products for the appropriate markets.

We will frequently use the expression "CIDM/QFD" because CIDM is about making Quality Function Deployment results possible and rewarding.

The essential focus of CIDM is described in figure FM.1. This graphic describes the flow of solution development from the setting of corporate strategies (this process was the subject of author Bill Barnard's first book, *The Innovation Edge*, co-authored with Thomas F. Wallace) to enhancing and supporting the final solution.

CIDM/QFD is involved in setting the overall action strategy, business action planning, program planning, and requirement planning. QFD is used as part of the design specification, development and testing, and enhancing and support phases—as well as the core foundation process for CIDM.

Figure FM.2 describes the actions encompassed in CIDM/QFD and graphically defines the boundaries of part III of the book. Part III is the "process" description of CIDM, primarily of the Quality Function Deployment (QFD) process.

Figure FM.1

CIDM/QFD and Its Fit to the Planning and Solution Realization Process

Planning Process			Solution Realization Process				
CIDM/QFD			CIDM/QFD				
"The Management Product"			"The Company Product"		QFD	QFD	QFD
Overall Action Strategy	**Business Action Planning**	**Corporate Objective Setting**	Phased /Gated Review Process				
			Phase 0	**Phase I**	**Phase II**	**Phase III**	**Phase IV**
Macro Resource Allocation	Business Plans	Strategic Issues	Program Planning	Requirement Planning	Design Specification	Develop and Test	Distribute, Enhance, and Support

The book is set up to support three levels of information transfer:

Part I. A high-level discussion of issues, for senior executives, that is designed to help them understand the reasons to support a CIDM/QFD; and make good decisions about where, when, and how to introduce CIDM/QFD; and clarify the roles they would need to play as leaders of the effort.

If an executive has no knowledge of QFD and feels the need for some detail about QFD before getting into the issues, then we recommend reading pages 115 to 126 and/or pages 215 to 218 before reading part I and part II.

Part II. This part provides some background knowledge on the issues confronting upper, middle, and project managers. We recommend that if the reader doesn't have a knowledge of QFD he or she read pages 115 to 126, and 169 to 189 and 205 to 218 before starting part II.

Typical Outputs from the Phases of CIDM/QFD and QFD

CIDM/QFD

The "Management Product"— Subject of the book *The Innovation Edge*

Market Identification

        Project Agreement   **Focus of Part III**
        Segment Identification   **of this book**
        Strategic Characteristics / Prioritization
        Value Delivery Promise Decisions

The "Company Product"

    Market Identification

    Project Agreement

    Customer Identification

    Strategic Characteristics / Prioritization

    Value Delivery Promise Decisions

"Value" Characteristic Prioritization
Competitive "Choice-based" Importance Understanding

QFD

    Quality Characteristic Analysis

        Function Analysis
            Component Analysis
            Technology Deployment Analysis

        Production Technology Analysis
            Function Analysis
            Component Analysis
            Technology Deployment Analysis

        Cost Analysis
            Function Analysis
            Component Analysis
            Technology Deployment Analysis

        Reliability Analysis
            Function Analysis
            Component Analysis

The subjects covered in part II are:

- The enhanced quality model.
- The difference between "choice" and "satisfaction."
- Quality and the evolution of Quality Function Deployment.
- The need for CIDM/QFD—the marketing war.
- Value delivery differentiation.
- The CIDM/QFD "expectations ladder."
- Understanding how CIDM/QFD contributes to success.
- Numerous "checklists" to be used by CIDM/QFD leaders in preparing for CIDM/QFD projects.

Part III. The CIDM/QFD process is explained in detail in this part for those engaged in actually completing projects. If you are a reader in this group you may want to refer to part II for background information and/or use the data provided in part I when engaged in writing proposals to management for support on QFD and CIDM/QFD projects.

Ultimately the value of this book will be in direct proportion to the amount of work you put into understanding it.

Preface

It has been twelve years since North Americans began hearing about Quality Function Deployment (QFD), and today one can find a number of books and articles in English that deal with the subject. Most of these treatments focus on the methodology of QFD and provide little detail about the organizational context, leadership requirements, and practical details for successfully integrating QFD into a company's way of life. And our own direct experience since 1988 in promoting the adoption of QFD in both large corporations and medium-size organizations convinced us that the published material left a gap too large to ignore.

Our work is not simply about the methodology of QFD as it typically is taught and understood in the United States. It introduces a broader approach to QFD that we call "Customer-Integrated Decision-Making^{sm} (CIDM^{sm})." This CIDM approach includes a stronger focus on market research to determine the "choice" behavior of customers and on ways to deploy successfully the decisions a team makes on the basis of a QFD analysis. As far as we have been able to determine, the CIDM approach we describe is closer to the full vision of QFD held by Japan's leading QFD guru, Yoji Akao, than most U.S. understandings of QFD. Since our Customer-Integrated Decision-Making approach is QFD-based, we will frequently use the acronym combination CIDM/QFD when referring to it. We will also sometimes refer to our subject with just the term CIDM or the more well-known QFD.

Customer-Integrated Decision-Making

This book is intended also to serve as a guide for leaders who desire to build competitive advantage and can see the value of making CIDM/QFD a key element of their strategy for delivering superior value to customers.

The book's perspective stems from the experiences we have had within Hewlett-Packard and with other companies in introducing and implementing QFD. Approaches for using CIDM/QFD to empower and develop teams during the introduction, integration, and internalization of the CIDM/QFD mind-set and methodology will be discussed. Our information base stems from knowledge of more than two hundred projects and fifty companies. As mentioned above, we will provide guidance for leaders at all levels who would like to be successful in using QFD as a strategic element in transitioning their product and/or service development and delivery from a "technology-driven" paradigm to a "Customer-Integrated Decision-Making" paradigm.

To make QFD-based Customer-Integrated Decision-Making an integral part of one's processes for identifying market opportunities, defining and developing products (including service products), and producing and delivering them to customers requires sustained effort and consistent leadership from many quarters. We describe the level of understanding and the type of leadership required—from top managers down through middle managers, project managers, CIDM/QFD process facilitators, and project team members—in order to use CIDM/QFD to accomplish the change to customer-driven quality deployment and value delivery that is needed to be successful in a highly competitive environment.

The reader will also learn in detail how to acquire appropriate and useful "voice of the customer" (VOC) information. Good VOC information is an essential input to Quality Function Deployment. Customer-Integrated Decision-Making provides more than most publications on QFD about how to get the VOC (frequently, the literature provides little guidance other than to mention that customer visits, surveys, and/or focus groups can be used). Since a sound strategy and process for understanding the VOC are absolutely vital, significant effort in each QFD project should be aimed in that direction.

You may have noticed already that in the back of this book is a pocket containing a "Resource Guide" (whose periodic updates will be available from Barnard-Norman for a modest fee), as well as a demonstration disk for QFD/CAPTURE, a software package created to support the QFD process by making it easy to create, update, and manipulate the matrices that are part of the current QFD methodology.

These items are included because our goal is for this book to be your comprehensive interactive guide for using QFD as an element of your company's strategy for building competitive advantage. We mainly describe QFD's use in the comprehensive and structured approach that is Customer-Integrated Decision-Making. To this end, you have in your hands the basic elements you need for a successful start in your efforts with CIDM/QFD.

Your goal is to use CIDM/QFD as both a useful mind-set and a methodology to support a truly customer- and technology-balanced way of doing business. A diligent reading of this book and application of its guidelines will provide your company with practical and tested directions to make your product development results more profitable.

Our goal is to provide you with a road map. Specifically, you will understand:

1. Where and when CIDM/QFD is applicable.
2. How the CIDM/QFD process works.
3. Factors affecting successful implementation.
4. What to do to get started.
5. How to use this book to get additional information and assistance.

Your expectation as you start this book should be that you are embarking on a journey whose goal is the internalization of a "new way" of doing business. You will be starting a process to change the "product development" paradigm to one that integrates the voice of the customer and team-oriented cross-functional effort and puts a high priority on detailed up-front planning.

Using the CIDM/QFD approach should reduce "political" decision-making by assuring a customer-integrated focus. Following the book's guidelines, you ought to be able to improve your results in defining products that customers want and in developing empowered and effective teams.

The following "Guide to Using This Book" defines some key terms that may not be self-explanatory and describes the intent and intended audiences of each of the major parts and chapters.

Guide to Using This Book

We have tried to address the needs of the various levels of management and scopes of responsibility by providing three levels of treatment of Customer-Integrated Decision-Making (CIDM) and Quality Function Deployment (QFD).

The driving idea for the structure of this book has been the increasing levels of detail concerning topics related to CIDM/QFD implementation as one moves from part I to part II to part III. Thus, part I contains a high-level view for top and upper managers. In part II, many of the same topics introduced in part I are addressed with a more-detailed treatment in order go give middle managers and project managers the level of detail they need to decide how to proceed with CIDM or QFD. Finally, part III provides information and descriptions of key CIDM/QFD tools at a level of detail that is most suitable for project managers, team facilitators, and team members.

To give you a better idea of the structure of the book, the following summary indicates the target audience and purpose of each part.

Part I. Executives who are not aware of QFD and want an overview that can be understood in about an hour or less.

QFD project managers who are looking for background data for justifying QFD to management.

Part II. Middle managers who are being encouraged to use QFD by upper management and/or are seeing a request for resources from teams and who need to understand the processes in detail.

Project managers who are being asked by management to look into the QFD process and/or are contemplating the use of the QFD process and its recommendation to teams.

Team members who want more background on the QFD process and its use and expectations for results in order to provide status information for management.

Part III. Team members who will be required to complete a QFD project.

Resource Guide. Team members looking for project support information.

Appendices. Readers who want detailed information on key subjects that may have been introduced in any of the parts of the book.

Part and Chapter Details

Part I, "Executive Overview," offers a high-level overview to introduce executives and upper-level managers, and others, to Quality Function Deployment (QFD), along with key issues and strategies to consider when developing a CIDM/QFD environment in the organization. Chapter 1, "Introduction," addresses two key questions: "Is Quality Function Deployment something I should understand and then sponsor?" and "What is Quality Function Deployment?" "Bringing QFD into Your Company" is the title of chapter 2. Discussed here is the influence of your company's culture and values on your selection of QFD rollout approach; also covered are leader roles, integration of QFD with other preexisting processes, success factors and pitfalls, and training for QFD implementation.

Part II, "Implementation Context and Guidance for the Middle and Program/Project Manager," provides a second level of detail targeted especially for middle managers, project managers, and QFD facilitators. Its four chapters go into more depth on several topics introduced in chapter 2 of part I:

Chapter 3. "Quality and Customer Choice: Where CIDM/QFD Fits"

Chapter 4. "Making CIDM/QFD Work in Your Company"

Chapter 5. "Establishing the Infrastructure"

Chapter 6. "Details and Expectations for CIDM/QFD Leaders"

Part III, "The Project-Level Practitioner," provides very specific detail to guide the project manager and QFD facilitator. Chapter 7 addresses how to define a project in which QFD will be used, including the drafting of a "road map" and the setting of expectations for QFD use. Chapter 8, "Leading the Team's Implementation," describes the roles and responsibilities of project participants—the project leader, the QFD facilitator, and team members, and chapter 9, "Identifying Segments, Customers, and Competition," covers an extremely important preliminary phase of QFD unique to CIDM that focuses and positions the team for maximum value. Chapter 10, "Key Market Research Tools," describes tools and approaches for getting the kind and quality of input data for effective use of QFD. The material of these two chapters represents part of the unique contribution of this book to the QFD literature.

Chapter 11, "CIDM/QFD Essence: The Logical Chain of Decisions," provides detail concerning the use of the matrices in the QFD methodology. "Project Management and Evaluating Project Success" is the topic of chapter 12.

A summary chapter concludes the main part of the book. It recapitulates major points about CIDM/QFD and offers our closing commentary concerning present and likely future use of QFD.

Last, but not least in terms of likely usefulness, are the Appendices. Descriptions of some advanced market research tools and "work aids" like checklists can be found there.

A Small Historical Note

This book came about as a result of a contract acquired by Bill Barnard to write a follow-up to his earlier book, *The Innovation Edge*. From the beginning, he believed that a work of this magnitude and nature—it aimed to describe an integrated process—could not be written alone. Therefore, he solicited and received commitment for support from a colleague at Hewlett-Packard, Doug Daetz. Barnard's belief—he was a senior QFD facilitator at HP—is that Doug's early and consistent support of the use of QFD at HP was one of the reasons that HP is in the strong position it is today.

In a ceremony in California early on, Barnard and Daetz flipped a coin to decide who would be the first-named author. Daetz won. As they moved to complete the manuscript, both became aware of an obvious need, driven from both a scope and business reality, to reduce the individual work load by adding another author. This person was an obvious choice to both Barnard and Daetz: Rick Norman. Rick had become Barnard's business partner, and he and Daetz had collaborated for several years, along with Barnard, in the promotion of QFD at HP. Norman accepted Barnard's and Daetz's invitation to help finish this book in early 1994. As the last to join the author team, Norman accepted having his name listed third.

The bottom line is that no one author is more responsible for the success of this work—each deserves to be first in the listing.

Acknowledgments

The authors would like to thank many people. Our wives—Gisela, Brenda, and Michael—are the first people. This book project tested their patience frequently over many months, but they continued to support and love us all.

We have interacted with managers and individual contributors from hundreds of CIDM and QFD teams around the world, and we thank them for all that we have learned from them. These people—as individuals and as teams—have helped to define and prove the process described in this book.

Finally, we must acknowledge the many people involved in reading and commenting on this book as it took form. Larry Shillito from Kodak, Larry Gibson from Eric Marder Associates, John Edholm from Pierce and Stevens, Ron Weeks from CINCOM Systems, Steve Nelson from SENCO Fasteners Emerging Countries, Mick Holtzleiter from SENCO Fasteners Europe, and Cynde Block. They all had significant impact on the direction of this book.

The final product is only as good, however, as the team that is responsible for incorporating the comments and suggestions can make it. Therefore, we have to say that the direction given was very valuable, but the result is our responsibility and not a reflection of the direction given. The three authors, therefore, accept the responsibility for any shortfalls and acknowledge the positive as largely due to the contributions of our supporters.

Customer
Integration

Part I

Executive Overview

CHAPTER 1

Introduction

We believe that you are reading this book because you want to determine how involved you and your organization should get with CIDM/QFD. And, if you become convinced that CIDM/QFD can deliver powerful benefits in your business, you'll want to know how to be efficient and effective in implementing CIDM/QFD.

By the time you finish reading part I of this book, you should be able to decide whether or not to proceed with bringing CIDM/QFD into your organization and, if yes, where, when, and how to introduce and support it.

There is only one situation that gives you an excuse to abandon this book now and do something else:

You have no competition now and never will have (i.e., you're in a permanent monopoly situation), and your customers must, of necessity and for all time, continue purchasing your good(s) or service(s) in sufficient quantity that your company can continue to make adequate profit even in the face of cost inflation.

So, you're still with us. That must mean that your business environment, like that of almost all businesses today, is not one of permanently captive customers and no competitors.

Let's start by naming some critical problems and business issues that confront many product and service providers:

Market share is being lost to competitors.

Profit is down (maybe even negative).

Product development takes too long and is too costly.

New products are not exciting customers.

These and many of the other critical problems and business issues that you might name are interrelated. And often the "product generation process" (which includes product definition as well as product development) is the common link.

Consider the following scenario created to show the interrelationship of the above-listed "results" problems (loss of market share, lower profit, unexcited customers) and the "process" issue (a long and costly product development process). Picture the CEO of Middle America Corporation speaking to an assembly of employees:

"Customers are not excited by our products because the value they perceive our products to have (value equals benefit minus cost) is not superior to that of available alternatives for satisfying their needs and wants. Frequently, people in our target market segments tell us that they wonder if we really understand how and where our products are used, since some of our products fail to be a very good match with their needs. Even when our products appear to match their needs well enough to be considered for purchase, potential customers say that our products cost more than competitors' products without providing compensating benefits. For example, they are not more accurate, more complete, quicker, less costly overall, easier to use, or better solutions to their problems.

"Furthermore, they say that, in general, we seem to be about a year behind the competition in introducing our products. As a consequence, our potential for market share is limited by the fact that they have already started buying the product from our competitors before we enter the market. The product solution that reflects a poor understanding of customer needs and the long development time are keeping us at a disadvantage relative to the competition; we receive less revenue from sales and we have higher costs from extended development time. There's little hope for improved profit unless we improve our process for defining and developing products."

Figure 1.1 depicts graphically what the CEO just explained.

If you can see that an important underlying cause of your company's "results" difficulties is a competitively inadequate approach and system for defining and developing products and services, then taking a serious look at Quality Function Deployment (QFD) will be very worth your while.

Figure 1.1

Consequences of Not Having a Customer-Focused, Structured Product Definition and Development Process

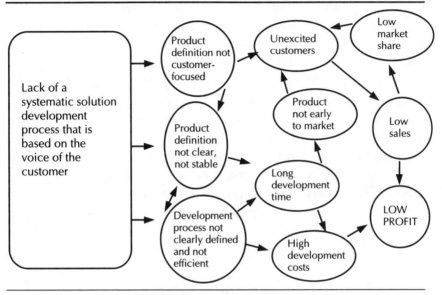

The principal purpose of QFD is to make sure that the needs and wants of customers drive the product generation process.

That's why we say that QFD starts with getting the "voice of the customer (VOC)," and why sometimes in the English-speaking world QFD is called "customer-driven product development" or "customer-focused design." In many places, QFD represents a break from several decades of predominantly "technology-driven" product development. As we will discuss later in parts II and III, the authors now prefer to talk about Customer-Integrated Decision-Making (CIDM) as the context for QFD because it more accurately focuses on the essence of QFD: integrating the customer needs into all company decision-making early. The first goal of QFD remains, as always, to avoid "market misses"—products that fail to win enough customers in the competitive marketplace.

A second major purpose of QFD is to improve the speed and efficiency of the development process.

QFD can reduce design time and engineering rework because it fosters team development of focused and explicitly documented product solutions, which tends to minimize extra "bells and whistles" and "personality-driven" changes to the product definition. A focused, stable product definition can save years of engineering design time and months to years of calendar time.

Some might add the breaking down of "functional silos" in an organization as a third major purpose of QFD, since QFD does promote and support the use of cross-functional project teams. Although there are cases we know of where the use of QFD did have the effect of largely breaking down the functional silos of the organization, at the overall organizational level, we see this as an incidental (but very beneficial) benefit and not one of the designed purposes for QFD's development.

Benefits of QFD

Before moving on to an overview of QFD, let's consider the benefits that, with your leadership, you should expect your organization to realize with properly sponsored, adequately supported, wisely applied use of QFD.

A way of looking at the benefits of QFD—or any approach, method, or tool—is to consider three different dimensions or perspectives:

1. *Scope/immediacy: Strategic benefits and tactical benefits*. Strategic benefits by definition have greater scope than tactical benefits, but generally take longer to be realized.

2. *Place: Internal benefits and marketplace benefits*. Internal benefits have their effect inside the company; marketplace benefits show up as increased sales, higher customer satisfaction, improved company reputation that will allow for a higher rate of retaining

customers, and a better ability to recruit top-notch employees, among other benefits.

3. *Measurability: Tangible benefits and intangible benefits.* Tangible benefits are those that can be measured—for example, reduction in the number of months to bring a product to market (time-to-market) or dollars of revenue above forecast; intangible benefits are benefits that one recognizes as having a positive effect but cannot measure in the present situation with present methods.

There are eight (two times two times two) possible combinations of these types of benefits. For example, one combination represents strategic, internal, intangible benefits. Thus, a company that sees their use of QFD helping to reorient their product generation process to one that has a greater focus on input from customers and on improving communication among marketing, R&D, and manufacturing personnel would be reaping strategic, internal, intangible benefits. However, the combination that short-run-focused corporate managers most want to see from any investment of human and other resources is tangible, tactical, marketplace benefits (for instance, higher sales and revenue from a newly released product).

QFD can provide such benefits, but for such marketplace success one must be prepared to wait until after a product (or service) has been defined, designed, produced, and put on sale.

Use of QFD can generate benefits that fall into all eight combinations of the strategic-tactical, internal-marketplace, tangible-intangible dimensions—but probably not all at the same time! Your business needs, company culture, and perhaps other factors will determine the type of benefits you need to pursue in the short term (e.g., internal, tactical, tangible/intangible benefits to maintain momentum in your introduction of QFD into your company) and in the longer term (e.g., tangible, marketplace, strategic/tactical, like increased sales and market share for a product or family of products). Table 1.1 shows many of the benefits of QFD reported by teams and organizations that have used it.

Do you see that your organization has a strong need for some of the benefits listed in table 1.1? By the time you reach the end of this

Table 1.1

Examples of QFD Benefits by Type of Benefit

Strategic—Marketplace—Tangible	*Tactical—Marketplace—Tangible*
Higher percentage of products that find market acceptance (lower percentage of "market misses").	Higher sales of a new product.
	Higher market share in a customer segment.
Shorter time-to-market due to improved stability of product definition and more clearly and completely defined linkages throughout the definition-to-design-to-production process.	Increased favorable word-of-mouth advertising for a new product.
	Lower warranty costs due to fewer design flaws and manufacturing errors.

Strategic—Marketplace—Intangible	*Tactical—Marketplace—Intangible*
Improved company reputation for understanding customer needs and delivery of products/services that meet customer needs.	Increased willingness of customers to share their ideas for product enhancements and new products with your organization.

Strategic—Internal—Tangible	*Tactical—Internal—Tangible*
Higher percentage of employees skilled in market research and other means of acquiring and analyzing the voice of the customer and information about competitors and competitive products/services.	Higher real-time availability of documentation concerning customer needs, competitive information, and team decisions.
	Stability of product definition.
Improved rationality of decisions in product definition and product development.	Fewer engineering change orders and less design rework.
	Shorter design time.
	Shorter project completion time.
	Lower project cost.

Strategic—Internal—Intangible	*Tactical—Internal—Intangible*
More focus on customer needs when defining products than on trying to push a technology.	Better cross-functional communication.

Strategic—Internal—Intangible	Tactical—Internal—Intangible
More complete and more visible market, customer, and competitor information.	Better team understanding of customer needs and wants.
Breaking down of functional silos.	Explicit, focused, documented product definition.
The introduction into product development activity of a TQC "best practice" (QFD).	Traceability of any product or production process element back to the driving customer need(s).
	Better consensus on decisions.
	Higher team cohesion and morale.

"Executive Overview" section, you may conclude that one of the best things you can do to improve the way your organization functions and the results it gets is to learn more about CIDM/QFD (see parts II and III, the appendices, and back-of-the-book materials) and then sponsor and promote the "bringing in" of CIDM/QFD into your organization in appropriate situations and to the appropriate degree.

What Is Quality Function Deployment?

Quality Function Deployment (QFD) is a systematic planning process that was created to help a project team bring together and manage all the elements needed to define, design, and produce a product (or deliver a service) that would meet or exceed customer needs. The guiding principle of QFD might be stated as follows: *Capture the "voice of the customer" and make sure that you convert that customer voice into appropriate strategy, product, and process requirements.*

The "mind-set" of QFD can be summarized as belief in the importance of three imperatives:

Go to the customer.
Work cross-functionally.
Plan thoroughly up front.

As a combination of mind-set and methodology, QFD provides both the customer focus and the methodological framework needed to assure that the "voice of the customer" (VOC) is recorded, understood, translated into appropriate product and process requirements, and communicated to all of the team members and relevant company executives.

In addition to its focus on customer needs, QFD also emphasizes cross-functional teamwork. The QFD approach requires cross-functional teams—typically involving marketing, R&D/design, and manufacturing personnel for hardware products—in order to:

- Adequately collect and interpret input on the needs of customers, customers' perception of the company's competitive standing, and the company's technical assessment of its products compared with competitors' products;
- Understand both technical and psychosocial relationships among customer needs and the means to satisfy them; and
- Integrate all the significant factors into a winning product design and an effective production and delivery process.

In short, the use of cross-functional teams guarantees a more complete and balanced view of customer needs, the competitive environment, and the company's possible responses when defining, designing, and producing products and services. This approach will assure reduced cycle time and higher "delight" potential in our product solutions.

Having members of an appropriately cross-functional team communicate well with each other and make project decisions by consensus is an objective of QFD that QFD's process elements and display methodology—matrices and tables—work to achieve.

The main benefits of QFD's matrix/table methodology are that the matrices and tables:

- Make visible the areas where a product development team needs to acquire information in order to define a product or service that will meet customer needs.

- Bring together in a highly visual and compact form, with traceability back to customer needs, all the important data/information that a product team needs in order for it to make good decisions concerning the definition, design, production, and delivery of the product or service.
- Provide a forum for analyzing the trade-offs that come about from understanding the issues arising from *customer importance* and *competitive importance* data acquired.
- Store the plan for the product, that is, the results of the decisions that the team makes.
- Can be used to communicate the product plan to supporting management and others who will have responsibility for implementing the plan.

In broad strokes, full application of the CIDM/QFD methodology involves the following steps:

1. Develop an understanding and prioritization of strategic objectives and market segments that will provide profit.
2. Obtain customer requirements: Listen to the "voice of the customer" and extract and organize the data concerning customer needs and the degree to which the needs are currently being satisfied.
3. Generate technical requirements: Translate customer requirements into corresponding product technical requirements.
4. Define the design: Specify the product's parts and critical part characteristics.
5. Identify production processes: Specify the processes needed to generate the parts.
6. Establish production control requirements: Specify the measures to be taken to keep processes within required limits.

These six steps are incorporated into a popular four-phase model of QFD.[1] As shown in figure 1.2, the four phases are:

I. Product Planning: Customer requirements to technical requirements

II. Design Planning: Technical requirements to part characteristics

III. Process Planning: Part characteristics to process characteristics

IV. Production Planning: Process characteristics to production requirements

Figure 1.2

Four-Phase Model for QFD

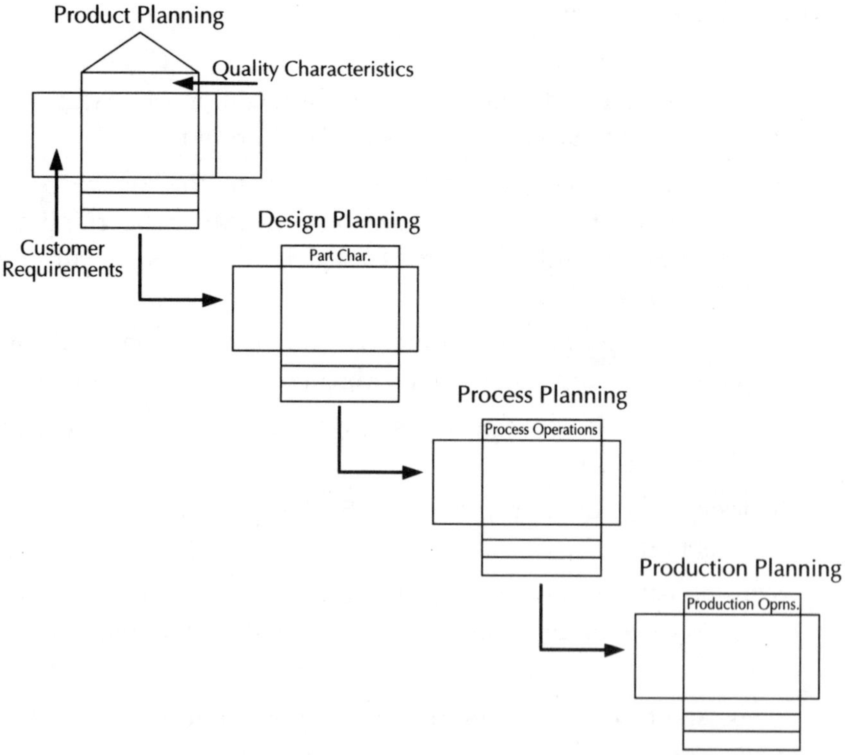

Product Planning

Quality Characteristics

Customer Requirements

Design Planning

Part Char.

Process Planning

Process Operations

Production Planning

Production Oprns.

Clearly, Phase I, Product Planning, is the phase with the most leverage. It's here that one has the opportunity to "define the right product." For this reason, most of the QFD work in the United States so far has concentrated on the Product Planning phase. Even in Japan, where QFD first came together in 1972 as a synthesis of "function deployment" (essentially, a value-engineering approach) and "quality deployment" and has developed and evolved over the last two decades, QFD effort focuses heavily on the Product Planning phase.

The matrix associated with the first phase, Product Planning, is often called the "House of Quality." Figure 1.3 shows the main "rooms" of a QFD House of Quality matrix. For example, information concerning (1) customer and potential prospect needs, (2) their relative importance, and (3) customer perception of and satisfaction

Figure 1.3

House of Quality

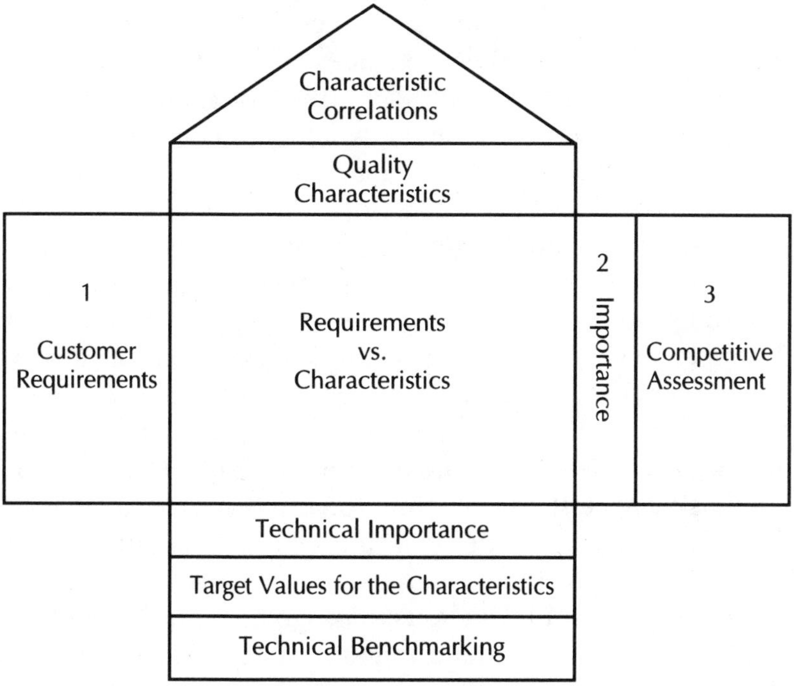

with existing/competing products. To help make the description of QFD more concrete, appendix I contains a fully developed example.

What are some of the first decisions I would need to make with regard to using CIDM/QFD?

The next chapter addresses the question of how to bring QFD into your company or organization. First, a few "executive decisions" with regard to use of CIDM/QFD have to be made.

The starting point is to have a clear understanding of the key problems of your business:

Am I losing market share to competitors?

Is my profit down (maybe even negative)?

Does product development take too long and is it too costly?

Am I releasing new products that are not exciting customers?

If any of the answers to the above questions are yes, then investigate the use of CIDM/QFD to solve these problems because it provides a process for determining what customers need and for converting knowledge of customer needs into products and services that customers will buy at a price allowing adequate profit.

A first step toward an appropriate use of QFD is the decision to develop some QFD knowledge and capability within your organization. You should start by having your key people read this book! For example, in 1987, the Corporate Quality Council at the Hewlett-Packard Company (HP) appointed a cross-functional task force—with people from HP's marketing, R&D, and quality communities, seven people in all—to evaluate the potential of QFD. After about six months' investigation, that task force recommended that the quality community move ahead with a QFD initiative to promote use of QFD throughout the company.

Before you decide to "get something going with CIDM/QFD," it is important to do some hard thinking about questions like the following:

1. The "goals for CIDM/QFD": What would I like to accomplish? What kind of benefits am I looking for in what time frame? Can I live with the fact that in the short term, the CIDM/QFD benefits may be primarily internal and intangible and that tangible marketplace benefits will only be realizable after a complete cycle of product development gets products to the market?

2. The "domain of application": For what kinds of activities do I want to use CIDM/QFD? Strategy development? Product/project portfolio selection? Product/service development?

While CIDM/QFD can be used in all three areas, applications to date and publications describing QFD have been predominantly related to product/service development. (See William Barnard and Thomas F. Wallace, *The Innovation Edge*, for CIDM/QFD applied to strategy development.)

If CIDM/QFD is to be used in product/service development, are we principally interested in Phase I, Product Planning, applications, or do we want to see CIDM/QFD carried into Phases II to IV?

3. The "extent of application" question: What is our current commitment to CIDM/QFD? Experimentation in a single area? In multiple areas? Or internalization/institutionalization (i.e., even if the champion goes away, QFD continues) in a single area or division? Across the company?

It is generally better for the organization if management decides to expand the scope of commitment if the results of using a new approach—in this case, CIDM/QFD—are positive, rather than to shrink the scope in the middle of the rollout. However, it is absolutely critical that, whatever the scope of the initial commitment, "constancy of purpose"[2] be exhibited by the sponsoring managers long enough for QFD to get an adequate trial.

CHAPTER 2

Bringing QFD into Your Company

Company Culture Considerations

To be successful with a go-to-the-customer, cross-functional, plan-ahead approach like Quality Function Deployment, one has to be prepared to adapt QFD to the company culture, or perhaps even the company culture to QFD.

Let's look at some of the dimensions of company culture that have a bearing on a possible approach to introduce QFD, use it successfully, and spread its use in the organization or company.

1. THE "IMPLICIT POWER" DIMENSION

What is the balance of power among the functional areas? Has a particular functional area historically or culturally controlled the decision-making? That is, when push comes to shove in major decisions of strategy and allocation of resources, does that functional area usually get its way?

In many high-technology companies, R&D does. If this is the case, there may be a need for selling the idea of spending money for market research and customer visits to get a more precise understanding of customer needs. There may also be a need to start building up capability in marketing and to establish more of a balance of power between R&D and marketing.

2. THE "AUTHORITY STRUCTURE" DIMENSION

Any organization has both a formal, or "official," authority structure and an informal, not explicitly stated or officially recognized, authority structure. While it is not so important to spend time differentiating between formal and informal authority in order to implant QFD successfully, it *is* important to know what kind of authority will be operating in the environment where QFD is to be used.

Does authority flow downward according to a strict and formal hierarchy? Or is authority based on a matrix of task-related roles, where, for example, for a particular project or program a person higher in the formal organizational hierarchy might report to a person lower on the organizational ladder? Or is the culture one where employees recognize authority based on knowledge, or seniority, or informal relationships? Or is authority vested in teams that make decisions on the basis of consensus.

At a broader level, do the divisions accept the authority of "corporate," or do they feel they have the liberty to ignore practices recommended by corporate groups? IBM has been, at least until recently, an example of the first situation, while HP has tended to typify autonomous decision-making.

When deciding on a plan for introducing QFD and spreading its use, one should take the type of authority structure strongly into account. For example, if the sponsor for QFD is near the top of an organization that operates with a hierarchical authority structure, and this person makes a decision to invest resources to bring QFD into the organization, then the possibility of rapid and widespread introduction of QFD may be quite good. On the other hand, if the sponsor for QFD is a project manager in a division in which decisions are made by consensus, it might take some time to develop the support to have one project team use QFD on a trial basis.

3. THE "ORGANIZATIONAL" DIMENSION

Unless your company or organization fits under one roof—or maybe two or three small roofs on the same site—you should consider the "organizational dimension."

Is the company highly centralized with strong corporate functions and highly subordinated divisions? Or is it decentralized, with highly autonomous, geographically scattered divisions that are responsible for different product/service areas?

Considering the two organizational extremes suggested above, it should be reasonably obvious that the spread of QFD could potentially be quite rapid in the first case and would most likely be difficult and slow in the second case (which will affect the product solution results in the marketplace).

4. THE "MANAGEMENT STYLE" DIMENSION

It is useful here to differentiate management style from authority structure. One key aspect of management style that is relevant here is whether it is a directive command-and-control approach or a nondirective empowered-employee approach. Another important aspect of management style is the degree to which it is short-term-results oriented in contrast to being planning-and-process oriented.

In an organization in which the culture supports a nondirective management style, managers cannot really "order" employees to do things, especially as related to the *way* the employees should do them. Instead, they must be able to "sell the benefits" of any new approach, tool, or methodology to their employees. Thus, in the case of QFD, managers who want their employees to try it must be able to make a convincing case for the benefits to be gained by using QFD. If the management style is both nondirective and highly short-term-results focused, then the selling of QFD may be very difficult until credible examples of QFD applications with good short-term results can be cited.

When the culture and management style emphasize planning and process, it is easier to create support for QFD without a lot of quantified data on benefits that will be realized; both managers and employees are more likely to appreciate the many potential strategic and tactical, tangible and intangible, internal and marketplace, benefits of QFD on the basis of its being a structured, customer-focused, cross-functional process that emphasizes up-front planning.

5. THE "WORK STYLE" DIMENSION

Several other aspects of an organization's culture might be rolled into a dimension called "work style." Specifically of concern here are the predominant attitudes and extent of formal and informal support with regard to:

Teamwork.

Cross-functional work.

Learning/education.

Employee empowerment.

From your reading of chapter 1, it should be clear that positive attitudes and belief in the process for these aspects of work style are "success factors" for the use of QFD. In the United States, where a cultural value is individualism, it is hard to be successful with QFD unless the host company or organization has been able to superimpose a value—and reward system—for teamwork and for working cross-functionally.

In the following sections and in the more detailed discussions of parts II and III, the significance and places of specific impact of the above dimensions will be made clearer.

QFD Rollout Models

The final section of chapter 1 discussed the question: "What are some of the first important decisions I will need to make with regard to using QFD?" The answers discussed there are a prerequisite for this section.

We will continue to assume that after some investigation, perhaps done by you personally or by a special investigative task force, you conclude that there will be significant business benefit in using QFD for strategy development, product/project portfolio selection, and/or product/service definition and development. You have decided that you want to bring QFD into your company or organization. If you haven't done so already, you need to answer questions like the following:

Where and to what extent shall we use QFD?

Is our goal to embed QFD into the way we do things, or to demonstrate that QFD is a method that is available?

It is only after arriving at answers to these questions that one should try to answer the following implementation or "rollout" question: What is the best approach for introducing QFD into the places we want to try it or establish it?

EXPERIMENTING WITH QFD

If your current commitment is only to "experiment" with QFD, then, of course, you would pick one, two, or a few selected projects to use a QFD approach and evaluate the extent to which the conduct and the results of the projects delivered benefits superior to those of prior approaches. For each project, the sponsoring managers and key project participants (particularly including the project manager) will road-map how far the QFD methodology needs to be taken.

The sponsoring management group will need to adequately support these pilot projects by providing training in QFD for participants and a QFD process facilitator. They will also need to provide adequate time (calendar time as well as dedicated staff time) and resources (money for acquiring "voice of the customer" input) in order to assure a fair trial of the QFD approach.

There is significant value in letting the organization know that experiments in using QFD are being undertaken. It is wise, however, to avoid giving a lot of "hype"—avoid such statements as "We expect great results from these projects." For many reasons—including factors beyond the project team's control or those not related to any inherent property of QFD—the initial projects may turn out inconclusively or even be perceived by some to have negative results. If this is the case an objective should be to identify what caused the projects to be perceived as less successful. These "partial" successes will help us to identify shortfalls in the over-all company and cause us to initiate additional experiments. Not predicting fantastic results from these first efforts will make it easier to move forward.

INTERNALIZING CIDM/QFD IN THE COMPANY

Now let's look at the situation in which your commitment is beyond experimentation; it is to bring QFD into use—ultimately, to make the QFD approach the way things are done—in the activities in the organization where you feel QFD will result in improved process and results.

Whether your choice is to use QFD for strategy development, product/project portfolio selection, or product/service definition and development, some of the main options with respect to scope and scale of your organization's rollout of QFD are:

Corporate rollout: Company-wide, multidivision company or multinational. For any area where the targeted activity, e.g., strategy development or product generation, is done.

Division or sub-division rollout: In one or a few divisions or departments. In a few areas, where product development is done. In particular subareas like the development of services. In a "verti-cal slice," e.g., in one division, using QFD from the top level of strategy to product development down through the subassembly and component levels. This could include asking suppliers to use QFD for their product development.

Selected projects: A small number of projects would be selected according to the following criteria: By importance of the application area to the business, willingness of host management and project team to use QFD, ability to provide necessary resources and infra-structure support, or likelihood of a successful outcome.

Using the five dimensions of culture introduced earlier as a backdrop, table 2.1 shows the cultural situations in which each of the above three approaches would have a significant chance of success.

Table 2.1

Company Culture and Choice of Rollout Approach

Implicit Power	Authority Structure	Organization	Management Style	Work Style
All functions have equal power	Formal hierarchy	Centralized, strong corporate functions	Directive	Cross-functional teams
Corporate Rollout				
Division Rollout				
Selected Projects				
One function has all the power	Informal authority (e.g., through knowledge)	Decentralized weak corporate functions	Nondirective	Individualism

Rollout Model Options

Culture Dimensions

NOTE: This table was suggested by Lianne Getz, an organizational development specialist at Hewlett-Packard Company, in Palo Alto, California.

ROLLOUT DECISION FACTORS

Factors to be considered when designing a CIDM/QFD only rollout approach include:

Positioning: For the targeted activities, will the use of CIDM/QFD be mandated, strongly recommended, or simply suggested?

Resources: What is the size of the budget that you are willing to commit for infrastructure support resources, and how long will the support budget continue?

Culture: How strong is the "not-invented-here (NIH)" response in the targeted groups? How prevalent is the "prove-it-to-me-first" mentality, in contrast to an "explorer" mentality?

A corporate rollout seeks to impact the whole organization. It requires the highest level and most stalwart management commitment. Because of its ambition to change the way one or more major activities are practiced throughout the company, it is the approach that is most likely to encounter areas of strong pushback. This most often is due to the NIH response. Also an issue can be the "prove-it-to-me-first" reaction. Such reactions are to be expected if the program is made mandatory or if there is no "phased" strategy. With a phased approach, participants in the first phase are either willing volunteers or people who have been identified as positively oriented to try a new approach (innovators and explorers).

A corporate rollout approach would likely mean a large number of projects would be launched and under way at the same time. Consequently, this approach requires substantial infrastructure support. Key aspects of support would include program management, training, QFD process facilitators, and QFD computer software. The approach of "mass training" should still be avoided in favor of just-in-time training for each team.

Companies that have used a corporate rollout approach include Hewlett-Packard, ATT/NCR, Raychem, and Motorola. At each of these companies, the QFD approach was included as part of a major initiative to improve product development. At other companies, like Ford, it was carried even to their suppliers.

The "selected projects" approach is at the other end of the spectrum with respect both to short-term ambition and resources required. It has the advantage of being a focused effort that does not require a large resource commitment, in comparison with the corporate approach. The small number of projects selected can be nurtured carefully to help ensure that they will be successful. Teaching participants about QFD can be handled easily with project-specific just-in-time (JIT) training, and the organization will need only a small number of facilitators to help the teams use the QFD process. Also, only a small number of QFD-assisting PC-based software packages would be needed.

Although the "selected projects" approach is the one that the authors tend to favor in most circumstances, because it seeks to guarantee early successes by focusing on a small number of projects that can be adequately supported, few companies are known to have consciously chosen it as their strategy.

The "division or subdivision rollout" approach falls in the middle between the "corporate rollout" and "selected projects" approaches, and it seems to be the procedure most often used. It was the way Texas Instruments' (TI's) involvement with QFD began; the divisions in TI's Controls Group in the Greater Boston area embarked upon QFD as a result of strong promotion by the vice president of the group. After some projects in the divisions of this group were successful with their use of QFD, "pull" for QFD from other divisions of TI in Texas and elsewhere was generated. A similar case is that of the 3M Company, where the first significant efforts involving QFD occurred in the Office Products Division (where Post-Its are made); again, word of successful use of QFD in that initiating division generated "teach me" requests from other divisions of 3M.

Whether one decides to follow a "corporate" "division or subdivision," or "selected projects" rollout approach, it is crucial to remember that committed and sustained management sponsorship— which means provision of adequate resources **over a multiyear period** and ongoing interest in progress and results that is evident to participants in the QFD-using activities and to other "watching" employees—is an absolute necessity for success in embedding the QFD approach into the targeted activities of the organization.

Technology Adoption Mechanisms

Many investigators over the years have studied how new technologies first get adopted and then spread to more users. One of the models of technology adoption that has been around for at least thirty years postulates that among the members of any human population, the tendency to adopt a new technology is not equally distributed; a small number of individuals exhibit a high readiness to try out new ideas, a larger number are willing to adopt a new technology relatively quickly after evidence shows it to be beneficial, a significant number will adopt the innovation a little later when the evidence of benefit is incontrovertible, and a small number will be very late adopters, if they adopt at all.

It is common to use the "bell-shaped curve" of the "normal" probability distribution to illustrate the way a population distributes itself with respect to "time to adopt an innovation." Figure 2.1 shows a typical characterization of the relative numbers of innovators, early adopters, early majority, late majority, and laggards.

At the beginning of the 1990s, a marketing professional named Geoffrey Moore put forth a significant new idea to help explain why the adoption of innovations frequently did not follow a pattern of smooth or continuous diffusion from innovators to early adopters, from early adopters to early majority, and so on. Moore said that the distribution shown in figure 2.1 should be drawn to show a gap (a blank space) between each of the types of adopters. These gaps would remind us that some specific things must occur or be done before an innovation would spread from one adopter group to the next one (moving to the right on the "time to adopt an innovation"

Figure 2.1

The Distribution of Individuals in a Population According to the Time to Adopt an Innovation

Innovators

Early Adopters

Early Majority

Late Majority

Laggards

Smallest time
to adopt an innovation

Longest time
to adopt an innovation

NOTE: Figure 2.1 adopted from figure (page 12) in *Crossing the Chasm,* by Geoffery A. Moore (HarperBusiness, 1991).

axis). According to Moore, the two most critical gaps for technology products—and QFD fits here as a technology product—are between the innovators and the early adopters, and between the early adopters and the early majority. This second gap is so significant that Moore calls it a "chasm."

So, in rolling QFD into your organization, it is important to recognize these "gap" barriers to adoption of the QFD approach—and to plan for a way to bridge them. For example, in order to move QFD from the "I'll try anything once if it sounds good" innovators to the early adopters, you've got to understand what early adopters are looking for. To quote Geoffrey Moore in *Crossing the Chasm*:

> [T]he key to winning over this segment [early adopters] is to show that the new technology enables some strategic leap forward, something never before possible, which has an intrinsic value and appeal to the nontechnologist. This benefit is typically symbolized by a single, compelling application, the one thing that best captures the power and the value of the new product. If the marketing effort is unable to find that compelling application, then market development stalls with the innovators, and the future of the product falls through the crack. (Page 19.)

For QFD, the compelling benefit for the early adopters in your organization might be that QFD can help a team arrive efficiently at a clear and stable product definition derived from true customer needs.

Getting across the chasm between early adopters and the early majority is the more formidable challenge. Moore continues:

> What the early adopter is buying . . . is some kind of *change agent.* By being the first to implement this change in their industry, the early adopters expect to get a jump on their competition, whether from lower product costs, faster time to market, more complete customer service, or some other comparable advantage. They expect a radical discontinuity between the old ways and the new, and they are prepared to champion this cause against entrenched resistance. . . . By contrast, the early majority want to buy a *productivity improvement* for existing operations. They are looking to minimize the discon-

tinuity with the old ways. They want evolution, not revolution . . . good references are critical to their buying decisions. (Pages 20–21.)

Members of the "early majority" group will want you to give them details on "credible" success stories. That is, the success stories must be in organizations that they feel are sufficiently similar (e.g., in the same culture and/or in the same industry) and are achieving business success. Early in the rollout of QFD, it may be difficult to provide the type of QFD success story that will convince members of the early majority, particularly if they insist on a case where market success has been achieved. The organization they will find most credible is their own organization or a sister division of it, and if use of QFD is just starting, it might take one to three years before a project using QFD reaches the stage of providing a product or service to the market.

When planning how to introduce and promote the use of QFD in your organization, there are a couple of key points to remember from this discussion about the adoption of a new technology:

• The adoption of a new technology follows a "life cycle" that starts with the innovators in the population and proceeds, if it proceeds at all, through the early adopters, early majority, late majority, and laggards.

• There are "gaps" to be bridged to move a technology from one technology-adoption group to another; the gap between the early adopters and the early majority is so significant that it should be thought of as a chasm.

• The program to introduce QFD into your organization needs to include plans for getting QFD across the gaps; most importantly, these plans should recognize that it is likely to be unproductive to approach members of the early majority too early, that is, before you can show them credible evidence of QFD's effectiveness (examples where QFD was used with good success in situations similar to theirs).

Leader Roles

A chain of leadership, starting in upper management (if not at the CEO), is required in order to successfully bring QFD into the company or organization.

There are four key groups of leaders that we want to focus on. Three of these groups consist of people who are managers:

1. Executive or upper-level managers.
2. Middle or mid-level managers.
3. Program or project managers.

The individuals in the fourth group may or may not have positions as managers in the organization—in fact, initially, they may be people from outside the company who are hired to facilitate and train the project team—but they have a significant leadership role to play in making QFD successful. They are:

4. QFD facilitators.

Before describing the "leader" roles that we feel the members of each of the four groups need to perform in order for QFD to take root and yield fruit in the business, let's quickly review why sustained leadership from top to bottom is so important in the case of QFD.

First, QFD starts with the idea of going to the customer—that is, to people in the target market segments and in the organizations that participate in getting products and services to customers. This is done in order to listen for and observe their needs and wants. This in-context approach will require resources—both people and money—and expertise that typically exceed what an organization is currently investing to understand market and customer needs. Therefore, the chain of management must maintain a commitment to investment in market research and customer visits, as well as in strengthening in-house understanding of market research techniques and methods of processing customer input.

Second, QFD requires cross-functional cooperation over a sustained period (usually at least months, and often for two or more years). The chain of management must thoroughly understand the importance of the cross-functional team in QFD and must assure that appropriately cross-functional teams are formed and kept together in each major phase of the project.

Third, QFD emphasizes thorough up-front planning; the matrix methodology of QFD is principally a framework for seeing what the team needs to know and organizing the available hard and soft data so that the team can come to consensus and decide what needs to be done.[1] The management team, as a network, must be convinced of the value of planning in heading off downstream waste or disaster. It must then support the "front-end loading" of projects that is necessary to get the planning benefits that QFD offers.

The issue is: "Will the sponsors and leaders of a QFD initiative demonstrate with deeds and resources the required commitment to being customer-driven; cross-functional program or project teams; up-front planning?"

Initiating the use of QFD will test promptly the degree of management commitment in all three of these areas.

EXECUTIVES OR UPPER-LEVEL MANAGERS

A successful introduction and internalization of QFD requires leadership from executive or upper-level managers of the organization where QFD is to be used. In small or single-division companies, or where a "corporate rollout" approach is planned, the leadership of the CEO is essential; leadership by the CEO's management team is also extremely important. In multidivision organizations where a "division or subdivision" or "selected projects" rollout approach is planned, the top manager, typically a vice president or general manager of each of the participating divisions, needs to lead the QFD action in some important ways.

The most important leadership responsibility is to be an active and visible sponsor for the QFD efforts. As a sponsor, a key leadership task is to hold personally the vision of the benefits being sought through use of QFD—clearer, more customer-centered product definitions,[2] less rework in product development, and greater market acceptance of offered products, and to remind managers and employees regularly of the expected benefits.

Other roles of the sponsor include defining strategy, which may be done in conjunction with others on the management team, assuring that adequate time and other resources are provided, reviewing progress with QFD, and celebrating the success achieved by those using QFD.

With respect to reminding managers about the purpose and benefits of using QFD, and ensuring that adequate time and resources are available, the executive and upper-level managers need to pay special attention to the middle or midlevel managers.

MIDDLE OR MIDLEVEL MANAGERS

Middle or midlevel managers are a key link in the chain of leadership and management necessary for successful use of QFD. These managers directly control the people and resources required to carry out projects. They can make or break an effort to use QFD through their assignment or reassignment of project team members, their reasonableness or unreasonableness with respect to schedule, and their supply or withholding of funds for obtaining and processing the "voice of the customer."

Sufficient time and energy must be spent educating middle and midlevel managers about the benefits and requirements of QFD. Failure to do this is one of the leading causes of the failure of projects attempting to use QFD and of QFD's lack of success in taking root in the organization. Managers in all the major functional areas—particularly marketing, R&D, and manufacturing—must be included.

QFD is doomed to no more than an occasional project success if middle management in either marketing or R&D fails to support it.

First and foremost, middle and midlevel managers must be "sold" on the mind-set of QFD:

1. Go to the customer;
2. Work cross-functionally; and

3. Plan thoroughly up front.

They must understand that QFD's main goals—the "why" of doing these three things—are to achieve market successes, avoid "market misses," and eliminate unnecessary cost (e.g., prolonged development efforts and engineering rework). Next, the middle and midlevel managers must be made to understand the consequences of applying the QFD mind-set, namely, the commitments of financial and other resources, including staff, that they would need to make in order for a QFD effort to have a high probability of success. It is disastrous for a project team that is trying to follow the QFD process to be told that only a small fraction of the money needed to conduct customer visits and market research will be made available to them. This money is better spent now rather than "fixing" the product after it is released. It is equally disastrous to have one or more members of the "core" team yanked suddenly from the project or not be assigned to the project when needed.

Middle and midlevel managers must understand that using QFD, initially, may take a bit more time than a comparable past project. It will most often yield a better result, however. A team using QFD for the first time must go through a learning curve. Though in principle QFD is reasonably straightforward, there are some aspects of QFD that require the use of tools that may be new to the project team. These new tools are in-context customer visits, affinity diagrams, relationship matrices, and others that are discussed in this book. The team will have to learn how to effectively and efficiently discuss and decide about the nuances of terminology, concepts, and causal relationships. Also, some projects using QFD may take longer than other projects, especially in the early stages, because the team may be doing some things that previous projects omitted (to their peril). Most notable in this regard is the collection and analysis of "voice of the customer" (VOC) information.

To help a team use QFD more effectively, middle management can provide "infrastructural support." Two kinds of infrastructural support are specifically helpful to QFD efforts. First is facilitation. A good QFD facilitator assigned to help the team work through the QFD process can increase the chances for success significantly. Second is software. Some software packages, which cost a bit less than $1,000, have been developed specifically to aid in developing and documenting the QFD matrices (see "Resource Guide" section in the back of the book for more information). Though such QFD-specialized software is not absolutely necessary to apply QFD successfully (a certain amount of assistance can be gained using a simple "spreadsheet" program), it does help relieve some of the "drudgery" of QFD and allow the team to spend more time on things other than documentation.

From the foregoing, you can see that the ongoing support and commitment of middle and midlevel managers are crucial for the success of QFD and must encompass a period of years, not months. Their big opportunity with respect to QFD is to provide leadership to the project managers and to give them enough time and an adequate and stable supply of project staff, infrastructural support, and funding for acquiring VOC data.

PROGRAM OR PROJECT MANAGERS

The QFD mind-set hits the QFD methodology at the program or project level. Here, the leadership and management of the program or project manager (abbreviated: PM) make or break the effort to use QFD. In fact, if the program or project manager is not committed to using the QFD approach, chances of successfully using the QFD process are extremely small. On the other hand, if the PM is 100 percent determined to use QFD and make it work, chances of a successful outcome are excellent if he or she also has middle management and upper management support, and moderately good even with weak or spotty support from middle and upper management.

The PM has the responsibility for the detailed planning of the program or project. Selection of the team members for the program or project is usually totally or partially under the control of the PM. And, of course, management of the day-to-day, week-to-week, and month-to-month execution of the program or project, as well as reporting upward about project status, are responsibilities of the PM.

If the PM plans to use a QFD approach, then he or she has to make implementation decisions that are in accord with the QFD mind-set. With respect to the "Go to the customer" part of the mind-set, the PM needs to negotiate adequate time and funding for the initial phase of getting VOC data. For "Work cross-functionally," the PM needs to identify the members (or at least the qualifications) for an appropriately cross-functional team and convince the managers of the people desired for the team to make them available as long as they are needed for the program or project. Relative to the third piece of the QFD mindset, "Plan thoroughly up front," the PM has to garner support for the up-front (that is, early) assignment of team members to the program or project.

The program or project manager can make some other early decisions to enhance the likelihood of a successful outcome using QFD. One of these decisions is to arrange to have members of the project team trained in the basics of QFD. Training of the team can be done up front—say, with a two-day classroom course brought to the site (there are outside vendors who do this; there may also be some in-house resources capable of providing the training). Or training can be done a little at a time, just-in-time, as the team proceeds from one activity to the next. In either case, at the start of the program or project, the PM should present to the team a "road map" for the planned use of QFD.

A second key decision of the PM concerns the use of a QFD facilitator: Will the program or project have one or not? If the PM and the team will be using the QFD approach for the first time, we would very strongly recommend that the PM engage a QFD facilitator to help guide the PM and team through the steps of the QFD process (see part III, chapter 8, for a discussion of the roles and activities of a QFD facilitator). Even when the PM and/or most of the team members have had some prior experience with QFD, if the experience has not been extensive, the PM should enlist the services of a trained QFD facilitator to help the team execute the process smoothly.

More information and details about the QFD methodology targeted for the program or project manager are included in parts II and III.

QFD FACILITATORS

The fourth and final leadership role that we want to discuss is that of QFD facilitator. A person who can facilitate a team's use of QFD will improve greatly the likelihood of a successful application of the QFD approach, particularly in cases where it is the first time that a PM and program or project team are trying to use QFD.

Usually, a person who functions as QFD facilitator has no direct management authority, but receives authorization for his or her activities with the program or project through the program or project manager. In some cases, a manager higher than the PM may insist that a QFD facilitator be used, but the PM, even if he or she accepts a facilitator, still can control the kinds and amounts of participation that the facilitator will have with the PM and the project team.

A QFD facilitator may come from outside the organization, and initially this may have to be the case if no one inside the organization has sufficient background and training in the QFD methodology. Organizations that plan to implant QFD in their strategy and product development activities may want to train some in-house QFD facilitators. In the Hewlett-Packard Company (HP), as part of its "QFD initiative," a five-day QFD facilitator training program was developed to prepare employees with suitable backgrounds (experience in training, coaching, team dynamics) to become QFD facilitators. For in-house personnel, the "QFD facilitator" role need not be full-time unless QFD activity is quite high (in HP, the QFD facilitator role was part-time in almost all cases). What is important is that the people who serve as QFD facilitators have sufficient flexibility in the scheduling of their time. During the start-up phase of a project, the demands on the QFD facilitator are usually the highest. For programs or projects in the start-up phase, when planning with the PM and preparation for initial training and team meetings take considerable time, even full-time QFD facilitators find it difficult to attend to more than one program or project at the same time.

The QFD facilitator contributes knowledge about the QFD approach and specific methodological steps, as well as management of team dynamics. The facilitator has many roles, which can be summarized using the expression "PiGiSH": plan, guide, stimulate, and harmonize.[3]

If a PM plans to use a QFD facilitator, ideally the facilitator should be recruited at the start of the project so that he or she can participate with the PM as co-planner of the execution of the project.

Much more detail about the role of the QFD facilitator is given in parts II and III.

Integration with a Solution Realization Process

The largest process for determining what solutions customers want and then arranging for the creation and delivery of the solutions is what we will call the "solution realization process," or SRP. The SRP includes within it what most companies call the "product generation process" or "product development process."

Whether one prefers to stick with the notion that products are produced via the product development process, or to think that solutions are identified, generated, and delivered by a solutions realization process, there is some advantage to trying to integrate CIDM/QFD into the process.

One of the biggest challenges is to arrive at the point at which QFD is used as a matter of course, as "the way we do things around here," and is not seen as extra or "add-on" work.

Initially, particularly because QFD will be new to employees and generally will require them to do some things that they haven't done previously, following the QFD approach is likely to be seen as add-on work. Without trying to deny the feelings of employees, and without driving so fast as to be perceived as unwise or reckless, the chain and network of management leaders should maintain steady pressure to build QFD into the mainstream process of product development or solution realization.

To be content to let use of QFD be the choice of an occasional product development project means that neither the organization as a whole nor individual projects will realize many of the benefits of

QFD. For example, if the management team is not aiming to use QFD as the backbone of the product development process, then they are not likely to establish the supporting capabilities and infrastructure—for example, in-house market research and QFD facilitation expertise, systems for constantly collecting and storing customer and competitor data, and "groupware" to facilitate the storing and sharing of information among team members—that help a project team to be successful in using QFD. The lack of a supportive context would mean lowered efficiency and effectiveness of each individual project team, for each team would have to find or create for itself the means to carry out the QFD approach.

Approaches to integrating CIDM/QFD into the product development process are discussed in part II.

Success Factors/Pitfalls/Corrective Actions

Some of our views concerning success factors and pitfalls for the use of QFD have been sprinkled throughout the earlier sections of this chapter. Based on our experience with several companies' efforts to introduce QFD, we can summarize the success factors in terms of six categories:

1. Management understanding and commitment.
2. Marketing input.
3. Training in the QFD methodology.
4. Supporting infrastructure.
5. Choice of appropriate projects.
6. Limiting the size and scope of first QFD efforts.

A lot has been said already about the need for management understanding and commitment. One thing that has not been stressed previously is that the success of QFD is enhanced if the organization where it will be introduced is one that is strongly committed to quality—is working hard to be a "total quality management" or "total quality control" organization. Where the organizational context is one of data-based decision-making and continuous process improvement, the QFD approach is likely to be more readily appreciated.

The second category, marketing input, is one that receives a lot of attention in parts II and III. As with most other processes, with CIDM/QFD, the quality of the output is limited by the quality of the input. Input from customers and the market is what initiates and drives the QFD process. Therefore, marketing input that is specific to the relevant market segments, provides sufficient data on customer needs and customer perception of competing products, and if available early in the project contributes greatly to successful QFD outcomes.

The third category, training in the QFD methodology, receives attention in the next section. For best results, the training should be available on demand with a short lead time, be sufficiently low in cost (in both training time and cost charged per participant), have appropriate content (e.g., relevant examples) and training methodology (e.g., hands-on practice) and a good reputation.

Two key aspects of supporting infrastructure—QFD facilitators and computer software tools—have already been mentioned. A third success factor is the provision of sufficient project space—a room dedicated to the use of the program or project team, where all the customer input and other data and the QFD matrices can be worked on and kept on display. Many companies refer to this as a "war room." It is where the "competition war" is planned and put into motion. It even begins to look like a war room after a while, with charts, and maps, and positions-oriented data. And it does make a good place to "brief the top brass."

The last two success-factor categories are somewhat related. The projects selected should have as many favorable starting conditions as possible: the project manager and the team want to use CIDM/QFD, the project is not large and its schedule is not too tight, and the project is important enough to management to stay funded and staffed but is not a "betting the farm" situation. Programs or projects selected should have clearly specified and limited objectives (for example, use QFD for the product planning phase and establish the definition of the product based on development and analysis of a "House of Quality" matrix; avoid objectives like "hit a home run in the marketplace" for initial projects). The number of projects undertaken at the start should not exceed the organization's ability to nurture them to successful conclusions.

For the most part, common pitfalls are: failure to build adequate management understanding and support; beginning projects without the team being trained and without a QFD facilitator; taking on too many projects or projects that are too big; and failing to go to customers to learn what they really need and want.

Clearly, corrective actions will involve the establishment of the success factors to counter or surmount the pitfalls and barriers that exist or are encountered.

TRAINING

While one can read an article or a book to get an idea of the basic concepts and methodology of CIDM/QFD, there is no substitute for trying to apply the approach to a real development problem for a relatively simple object like a pencil, pizza, or oil-change service. CIDM/QFD seems conceptually straightforward when one reads about it, but, in practice, it confronts a team with many nuances and points of interpretation.

We find a useful analogy in business accounting. Rick Norman uses this analogy quite often in explaining the "nuances and points of interpretation" to novice users. CIDM/QFD is like accounting in that the "practice" of doing it concerns itself with *applying principles* to business situations. Just as accountants apply "generally accepted accounting principles" to a business to assess its financial condition in order make financial decisions, CIDM practitioners apply "generally accepted CIDM/QFD principles" to a business to make product development decisions. The amounts of time that it takes to become proficient in knowing how to apply these sets of principles are somewhat similar. Even with internal accounting departments, companies still find it useful to use specialized "accounting firms" to help prepare annual audits of its financial systems. Likewise, we envision a time when specialized CIDM/QFD firms will help companies on a regular basis update the health of their product development systems.

A team trying to do QFD without training—especially if they also do not have a QFD facilitator—is a team with a high probability of disintegration or failure. Basic training that addresses "what QFD is and how you do it" should be provided to the PM and team members either at the start of the program/project or in stages on a just-in-time basis. This training should be workshop-based as much as possible so as to give the future QFD users a bit of experience in applying the QFD methodology.

Generally, it is better to provide QFD training to "intact teams" so that part of the training can be tuned specifically for their project; for just-in-time training, intact-team training is effectively the only option. If the decision is to provide a relatively complete training experience at the start of the program or project, then classroom training that includes people from other teams (and/or members of the "extended" program/project team) is an option that may be more cost-effective. One can successfully support a core project team that has five to twelve members.

The previous paragraphs address what might be called "basic QFD training"—what QFD is and how you do it. In the discussion about QFD facilitators in the earlier "leader roles" section, "QFD facilitator training" was mentioned. The training for QFD facilitators needs to include the basic QFD training, but also must include "outside expert" facilitator mentoring through the first effort. This will go beyond "basic training" and build additional understanding and skill in many of the more difficult areas of the QFD process and in managing team dynamics (see part III, chapter 12, for more detail).

But there is a third kind of training that is also vitally important. It is training that is too often overlooked, but it is so important that not doing it could guarantee failure in your efforts to bring QFD into your company. This is training for all levels of managers—but it is especially crucial for middle managers—on how to implement a QFD program.

This book can be considered a response to our conviction that training and guidance for the management leaders are necessary for QFD to be successfully introduced into an organization. We suggest that the content of this management training should cover at least the main points of part I of this book, and for middle or midlevel managers also the main points of part II. For executives and upper-level managers, a one-day training session may be sufficient, and for middle or midlevel managers, as well as program or project managers, a training session of two days should allow sufficient time to introduce and discuss the main ideas and issues related to implementing QFD.

Additional information about the QFD training is provided in parts II and III. Information about sources of training is included in the "Resource Guide" at the back of the book.

Summary

Implementing CIDM/QFD in an organization is no trivial undertaking. Done effectively, it will have far-reaching impact. It should be viewed as a new, highly interactive way of doing the business of product development. When you really think about it, having a totally customer-oriented company makes good sense.

The role of management is absolutely key in assuring CIDM implementation success. CIDM implies doing things that the organization is not, most often, accustomed to doing. In fact, most organizations with which we are familiar don't have the skill sets or the mind-sets to sustain a CIDM environment.

Part II will address more of these management mind-sets that must be the leading thoughts for CIDM to achieve its goal: competitive advantage.

Part II

Implementation Context and Guidance for the Middle and Program/Project Manager

Introduction

The second part of this book will continue defining the "(Voice of the) Customer-Integrated Decision-Making" process in more detail. The objective is to provide for the needs of leaders, those who manage from many levels of responsibility and will be the major support for projects. They hopefully will be using the process themselves to better define their strategic objectives. This "customer integrated" understanding will assure realistic setting of expectations regarding the support required to assure success.

Chapter 3, "Quality and Customer Choice: Where CIDM/QFD Fits," starts by describing some "foundation issues." An understanding of these issues will provide leaders with the background to understand the importance of "customer integration." It starts by describing the notion of the "enhanced quality model," a more comprehensive quality than traditionally has been defined.

We also define a "robust product," which is a solution that is more than the product or service by itself. It is a "solution" that must be recognized by the "whole company" as the developer and deliverer. We call this comprehensive solution the BIG P and contrast it with a more specific product solution called the "little p." The importance of this difference is summarized in a discussion of the value delivery proposition.

The objective of QFD-based "Customer-Integrated Decision-Making," then, is the identification, understanding, and development of all of the dimensions and values that can be "differentiated" potentially in delivering a solution. This effort results in the most realistic solution for "products" that provide sustainable and competitively advantaged "value."

It's impossible to achieve consistent "market success" without discussing how customers evaluate differences and make "choices" in buying, to do so requires contrasting that with the notion of "satisfaction." Discussion on this topic focuses on the problems that come about when we just try to "fix what's not satisfying the customer" (we refer to this as working with "historical" quality). The difficulty occurs when one believes that this action alone will provide what is needed to cause customers to "choose" to buy. When one pays attention to why customers buy, that is, customer choice behavior, we refer to this understanding as developing "future" quality.

The next foundation issue discussed describes the importance of "customer integration" when moving from being "technology-driven" to "customer-integrated." We describe how to internalize a "mind-set" of Customer-Integrated Decision-Making (CIDM) within the enterprise. The expectations for this "mind-set" internalization are detailed and include the phased results to be expected, referred to as the "expectations ladder." Experience gained from having the responsibility for internalizing these processes by the authors at Hewlett-Packard, ATT/NCR, and Motorola. Facilitating experiences at these companies and Sun, Pierce and Stevens, SENCO Fasteners, and others are drawn on in defining these expectations as well.

We will spend quite a bit of time talking about the importance of and the requirements and responsibilities for teaming. Experience is that the CIDM/QFD process approach will develop a structured interaction among a company's various members. This action will support teams beyond the first level of integration, "work groups" (most often called "teams"), to true teaming efforts. Experience is that "true teams" are those that accept the responsibility for their actions.

The CIDM approach also very quickly supports third-level group integration—referred to as "high-energy adaptive teams (HEAT)." As leadership provides most of the support for developing the group interaction, we will define with some detail the support required from leaders and managers. We will include a list of questions managers should be concerned with asking periodically to ensure the results are occurring.

In part II, we provide a "next level of detail" project activity list. This list will identify the total number of days during a generic project that each of the team members could be expected to be involved in meetings. See appendix VIII, for a more detailed list of the approximate number of days that the company, in advance, will have to be prepared to support.

Chapter 4, "Making CIDM/QFD Work in Your Company," introduces the notion of a "solution realization process" and shows where the QFD-based CIDM approach fits in that process. It also briefly describes some of the more well-known alternative models of QFD.

"Establishing the Infrastructure" is the topic of chapter 5. One of the contributions of this chapter is a listing of potential training requirements that managers must consider as they evaluate the readiness of their teams. This will focus on the importance of "peripheral" training interventions as they relate to CIDM/QFD.

Part II closes with a chapter that addresses the roles of middle managers and project leaders and the expectations for their leadership in order for the organization to experience success in applying CIDM/QFD.

CHAPTER 3

Quality and Customer Choice: Where CIDM/QFD Fits

Preparing the Foundation

Before describing how the CIDM/QFD process is accomplished, we must understand some "foundation" concepts and principles. Part III will detail the process of using CIDM/QFD, but first let's look at these "foundation issues" before we explore the accomplishment of the methods.

THE "ENHANCED QUALITY" MODEL

Our "enhanced quality" model (shown in figure 3.1) describes the contribution of various tools, processes, and methodologies, including QFD, in meeting customer expectations and providing "benefit delight." Our model is a visual presentation of the effort to provide "quality." It applies to any form of "solution," whether it involves strategy, product, and/or service. Understanding these dimensions will provide a foundation for accepting the nuances of the CIDM/QFD process.

The authors' experience is that quality is created through the integration of three dimensions:

1. Traditional dimensions such as total quality control—we call this "functional quality."

2. The "voice of the customer" dimensions that QFD supports—we call this "choice quality."

Figure 3.1

Enhanced Quality Model

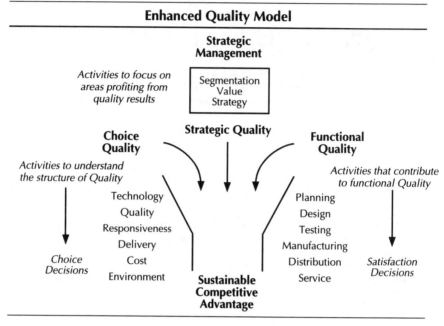

3. Customer-Integrated Decision-Making dimensions—we call this "strategic quality."

When these three dimensions are considered during decision-making, the leadership will be more effective when setting objectives. The enterprise will focus on defining the actions for more profitable markets. We use the term "management product" to refer to the deliverables from managers, namely, their decisions and actions that establish direction, objectives, and strategies for the organization.

We use the term BIG P to reflect the actions of the company that provide the overall solution for those strategic objectives.

Let's review each of the components in the "enhanced quality model." (The model builds on work done by Joseph Juran and Yoji Akao, an American and a Japanese quality expert, respectively.)

THE COMPONENTS OF "ENHANCED QUALITY"

Functional quality refers to the use of "quality assurance" tools, most of them referred to by the terms "total quality (TQ)" and "total quality control (TQC)." We use these tools to impact the "satisfaction" quality of the product. This is where we have historically used our satisfaction surveying efforts to understand the "product satisfaction" of the user. Satisfaction describes how well and consistently we have executed and delivered "expected product benefits."

On its own, functional quality will allow one to compete for "parity" with other products, but will most often not result in significant innovation.

Choice quality describes the effort to understand what the customers' meaning of value is. This goes beyond simple understanding of "satisfaction" described previously and demands understanding, in some detail, the "choice-making" processes of the customers. Attributes involved in choosing the best "benefit solution" from among available offerings might be those of functionality, usability, reliability, price, serviceability, financing, and delivery.

This effort is supported by processes such as "predictive models" and Quality Function Deployment. Success through the use of these tools has been demonstrated by companies such as Toyota and Hewlett-Packard. In this dimension, we work to understand, from the perception and perspective of the many users, the structural definition of the needs and benefits required to accomplish the *solution* required.

Work in this dimension goes beyond trying to understand how to simply "satisfy," to providing an opportunity to "delight and enlighten the customer."

Strategic quality is the initial dimension of quality, and the one most often overlooked; it is the effort on the part of management and the company to understand where they should pursue markets for its "solutions," in other words, where to "sell its products."

This form of strategic definition was developed by author Bill Barnard as the "management product." The "management product" is the defining of proactive "choice-based" integrated quality objectives and strategy definition efforts. Completion of a good management product will launch company action teams toward markets that have been defined as potential high-profit segments. Recognizing and understanding that there are three dimensions in achieving quality is important in developing the environment for achieving "sustainable advantage."

THE DIFFERENCE BETWEEN "CHOICE" AND "SATISFACTION"

One of the more contemporary aspects of "voice of the customer" understanding efforts is the need to evaluate the "voice" using data that represent the customers' choice-based perceptions of both the attribute importance and the competition's ability to provide the "want."

Traditionally, the objective of market research was to discover—usually from closed-end surveys—the attitude of the customers on how satisfied with the product they were. This, then, implied the customers' importance of these issues.

More recently, mainly in a few service industries and a forward-thinking electronics company like Hewlett-Packard, there has been a movement toward balancing this postdelivery effort with a presolution definition understanding of the importance customers place on wants and needs, based on their "choice importance perception." This approach seeks to predict the customers' "choices" on attribute and function preferences of the proposed solution. We work to understand how the customers will make their decision to "buy."

Larry Gibson, of Eric Marder & Associates, provides this insight into customer decision-making by describing the "choice decisions" customers could make. He calls this description the "cusp of choice."

Figure 3.2 describes the potential situation any solution provider is faced with in making decisions to focus on providing customer solutions. Customers present themselves to solution providers as one or more of these three:

1. They are our customers and we won't lose them easily through our actions. They could be customers that we have, but just narrowly—a small miscalculation on our part could lose them.

2. We don't have them but we could easily, or with relatively small adjustments, gain them as a customer.

3. We cannot do anything to acquire them—at least not without a prolonged effort.

Figure 3.2

The Cusp of Choice

Those customers we have and won't lose

– –

Those customers we have but could lose

Those customers we don't have but could win

} **The Cusp of Choice**

– –

Those customers we will never get

Companies will find that more profit is realized through making decisions that gain customers using important but small change efforts than through the "home run" efforts that "bet the company." The "cusp of choice," then, is making trade-off decisions that "lose the fewest customers while gaining the most." CIDM is about trying to know who they are before we test the solution in the market to find out!

The main important segments of customers we must worry about, then, are those within the "cusp of choice"—"those we have but could lose" and "those we don't have but could win." We have to decide how our decisions affect the "customers we could lose and could gain"—we must make decisions that cause us to gain more customers than we lose.

This requires identification of the customers and what decision-making processes they are using to "choose to buy."

We do research that helps us to understand how customers group, or segment, themselves in the markets, and what those segments of customers use to decide to buy a solution.

It seems, then, that customers often do not buy what satisfies them—they buy based on a set of "choice" criteria. The discovery is that customers often buy products that do not have all the "satisfiers" they demand in satisfaction studies—especially if they have a low priority in our "choice ranking."

Quality and the Evolution of Quality Function Deployment

Given all of the data discussed above, there are a number of dimensions to understand before we truly define what quality is. To date, our experience is that most companies do not have this complete understanding. This is an issue not only in America and Europe, but in Japan and other parts of Asia as well.

Most often, this is because the view of quality is one-dimensional, or at best two-dimensional. A three-dimensional understanding—strategy, choice, and functional understanding—is one that allows leaders a more robust perspective in making decisions. This impacts favorably not only on decisions, but also on who should be part of teams and what expectations should exist for a project.

Let's take a look at this notion of *quality* and its recent history.

In the book *Quality or Else*, Lloyd Dobyns takes the reader through a fascinating journey on the history of quality. He also describes in detail the issues on the how the Japanese define it.

One discovery the reader makes is that W. Edwards Deming and Joseph Juran did not "make" the Japanese "high quality" commercial product producers, but rather that Japan was already the quality leader. Juran, in a 1994 *Harvard Business Review* article, stated that Japan was already dominant, as exemplified in their art and war machines. Juran's conclusion was that he and Deming had simply accelerated the Japanese into becoming "consumer product" quality leaders.

The literature today is beginning to support the notion that a customer's judgment regarding "superior products" is based on many attributes, not just satisfaction. This book supports the need for an integrated, replicable process. This process must include considerations for all of the dimensions of quality.

Quality, therefore, is more than just some "training in tools and methods." A company must start someplace, but to succeed, the effort must be more than just improving *functional* quality.

Quality Function Deployment is both a tool set and a mind-set. It is often referred to as a "Japanese quality" process. A review of QFD's history, however, shows a different picture. QFD's development shows that what occurred over the years from 1966 till 1977 is a consciously planned effort to develop an integrated methodology to assure the integration of a company's marketing, engineering, and manufacturing organizations.

This approach would allow for the deployment of superior quality function and value-based cost into products to assure higher sales. The objective was to troubleshoot product problems in development rather than after release from production, to shorten the development cycle by working on the project in parallel, and, finally, to grow market share by providing high-quality, differentiated solutions.

What occurred from 1966 to 1977, and on into today, was a gradual integrating of various American quality tools into a linked process. What must be stressed is that the tool set used to accomplish QFD was developed in parts in America, and the methodology assembled in Japan as an integrated process.

CIDM integrates basic and advanced forms of American market research into the QFD methodology and expands the power and value of QFD.

The result is to fill an acknowledged shortcoming in "data reliability" of the QFD process. This is done with approaches like "in-context market research" and "customer choice prediction," thus improving the reliability of QFD decision-making. We will talk more about these in part III and this chapter.

Quality Deployment was the first form of this integration of tools; it was focused on design quality and the influence of the concept that "quality is the responsibility of everyone in the company," "not just manufacturing" (Ishakawa circa 1960). Its narrowly focused cousin Quality Function Deployment evolved next; it was concerned originally with the deployment of quality to people within the engineering and manufacturing quality efforts. The notion of QFD always has worked to integrate the customer and the company—CIDM/QFD evolves that goal further.

QFD, then, is an integration of American quality tools, such as quality assurance (QA), value engineering (VE), value analysis (VA), failure mode and effect analysis (FMEA), matrix charts and matrix diagrams, fault tree analysis (FTA), and tree diagrams. In the 1960s, the Japanese began an innovative integration of these quality tools by developing a mind-set and methodology for integrating both the company internally and then the company and the customer externally. A great reference on the history of QFD is the recently released book by Shigeru Mizuno and Yoji Akao, *QFD: The Customer-Driven Approach to Quality Planning and Deployment.*

CIDM is a further evolution that adds research tools and concepts that are very American to an American tool set that was evolved by the Japanese into a more customer-integrated process. Our model includes a "Third Quality Dimension," strategic quality—as described at the beginning of this chapter. The integration of all of these dimensions will lead to a fourth dimension of quality, that of adaptive leadership. This leadership approach will support leaders in fast-changing markets by providing knowledge on how to flexibly adapt to changes.

CIDM/QFD describes a powerful combination of tools, methods, and processes to support all the dimensions of quality, with a focus on the list found in figure 3.3.

CIDM/QFD assures superiority in execution of results, will decrease time to introduce successful products and impact team decision-making homogeneity and culture change.

Quality is not simply an overnight training "thing." Nor is it just an engineering "thing"—it is a state of mind and it has to encompass a number of events and actions that over time evolve to "quality."

The next section defines expanded quality and identifies those dimensions often not included in our traditional definition of consideration for quality.

Figure 3.3

CIDM Focus

- Integrating all three quality dimensions.
- Understanding and considering the "value delivery" proposition.
- Requiring "in-context" customer contact for want and needs data acquisition.
- Stressing the use of "choice prediction" importance understanding rather than traditional "satisfaction" and/or internally statistically derived importance definition.
- Use of the matrices as a data focusing tool for collection and analyses.

The Need for CIDM/QFD—The Marketing War

THE RULES OF "MARKETING WAR"

The rules in figure 3.4 are an adaptation of a "rule of war" made by the Chinese many centuries ago regarding the potential for success in battle. They come from *The Art Of War* by Sun Tzu.

Figure 3.4

Marketing Warfare

- If you do not know yourself (the customer issues and benefits required and how to use your competencies and/or work together as a team) and do not know your enemy (competition and the customers' perception of them, as well as technical comparisons)
—there is very little chance of winning a war.

- If you know yourself (the customer issues and benefits required and how to use your competencies and/or work together as a team) and do not know your enemy (competition and the customers' perception of them, as well as technical comparisons)
—there is a 50 percent chance of winning the war.

- If you know yourself (the customer issues and benefits required and how to use your competencies and/or work together as a team) and know your enemy (competition and the customers' perception of them, as well as technical comparisons)
—there is a very good chance of winning the war.

The CIDM approach supports internalizing information related to the success variables described in figure 3.4. More specifically, CIDM will support "knowing" and "internalizing knowledge."

KNOW YOURSELF—THE CUSTOMER AND THE COMPETITION

Companies using QFD and the CIDM process develop teams faster that are more understanding of customer issues. This is made possible through the use of in-context customer visits. As the principal method of data acquisition, these visits must be conducted with the participation of every member of the CIDM/QFD team. When the team is supported and truly multifunctional, with significant expertise from each of the value delivery contributors of the company, then the possibility of translating the "learning" from these visits into competitively differentiated solutions is much greater.

CIDM tools used in the way we describe them will help the teams to become more focused in these visits through the development of "choice-based" probing preparation. CIDM/QFD preplans the visit, using tools such as the "voice of value table (VOVT)." This table is designed to provide teams with the ability to presurvey the target segment for their "choice" focused importance of the value delivery of current solutions and the competitive perceptions they might have regarding anyone's ability to deliver the solution. It is used to preview the customer in an effort to develop meaningful question and probing focus for the in-context customer visit guide.

QFD, when used in the complete CIDM approach, will provide team members with the ability to appraise realistically their personal capabilities and value potential and/or the companies' process and resource potential to meet objectives. The process of setting "target values"—the values the customers use to know they are getting what they want, for "quality characteristics" will yield, through a complete interaction with the customer, both verbal and observational, a more realistic knowledge of those targets. In part III, we will detail a format that should be used to develop the "target value" based on the customer, the competition, and the companies' competencies.

KNOWING YOUR COMPETITION

The discovery power of QFD and CIDM is experienced as the teams acquire competitive data. These efforts to identify, often for the first time, who the competitors are, and the customers' perception of competition, are very revealing to the team.

This effort—as hard as it is to believe in the 1990s—has not been made extensively in the past. If it *has* been done, it was only for a very few competitors, from a "technical benchmarking" perspective. The "flaw" is that along with defining the solution from a technology view, the customers' feature function set has only been compared with the competition from an internal technical "reverse engineering viewpoint."

The "fatal flaw," then, is that companies assume what the customer wants and assume the importance based on satisfaction and an internal technical comparison of those feature functions. Companies are not considering the "choice"-based importance of the customers' value "benefit" needs and wants and are not including the customers' perception of the competition's ability to supply them with the solution in their decision-making.

Figure 3.5 is a worksheet with which you can review your company's readiness for "marketing war." This worksheet asks questions that after being answered will help you to comprehend the magnitude of your "knowledge" acquisition. They should be answered after careful consideration from a cross-functional team. The bottom line is that if the "team" is not in agreement on each answer, then there could be a problem with what we "think we know," and what we "actually know." Problems in leveling the team often show themselves in slow execution of the actions to accomplish the project, then product performance issues in the market place.

Knowing company strengths relates to "knowing the target value targets" and the "priorities of the attributes" and then deciding if we are putting the right resources to the right problems.

Figure 3.5

Marketing Warfare Self-Assessment Worksheet

Capability /Status	Segment 1	Segment . . . n
Do you know (not suspect) your company's strengths?		
Do you know (not suspect) your segment/customer?		
Do you know you have a viable *Little p?*		
Do you know you have a viable BIG P?		
Is there a "value" difference you can advertise?		
The answers to the above questions provide a basis for answering this last one:		
Can you define a sustainable competitive advantage for your solution?		

Knowing our competition's strengths is to know not only our customers' perceptions of our direct competition, but also the perceptions they may have of any supplier's ability to provide the solution.

Knowing our *Little p* is about knowing, not just having a feeling, that our solution provides the customer with at least the top three to five attributes they want. More importantly, there exist some differentiators for our solution over the competition. We must understand this from the "perception of the customer," not a "reverse engineering" effort.

BIG P solutions result by understanding our "value delivery proposition"—all actions we provide as part of the solution. This is where many companies find the "differentiators" that provide them with competitive advantage.

Knowing that our "answers" are true from the voice of the customer, not just "feelings," will allow us to decide if we have a sustainable advantage over the other suppliers in our market. We can then decide if we are fighting with "advantage" or "emotions."

We should answer these questions for many segments in an effort to find the "best battlefield in which to do business (war)." In our experience, "Winners pick the wars they can win."

After you finish the worksheet, read on about how the CIDM/QFD solution will help you overcome problems you may have discovered and/or admitted during your review.

WHAT DO WE NEED TO KNOW?

The following discussion is about the issues companies must consider in today's highly competitive marketplace. This is important as companies struggle with limited resource, higher "value" demands from customers, and more competitors. The first question facing leaders is, Where should I do business? The other questions address the reasonability of doing business in those markets—what will assure success, in profit.

Which markets offer the best possibility for making adequate profit, and which ones will require investment to gain profit?

One of the main issues in defining a strategy is first understanding the importance of the market/customer as the objective. Experience shows this is one of the big problems in realizing cycle-time reduction and profit maximization. The leadership doesn't always review the potential for success before developing its strategies, action plans, and solution plans. The need, then, is to spend time in a robust effort to define the reality of developing products that are measured on maximizing profit or just supporting investment efforts to gain market share over many years.

If the leadership has not done this planning, or if in the scheme of developing a solution realization process they have chosen to empower the product development teams to do it, then CIDM/QFD will support the accomplishment of this decision-making.

What is it that our product/solution offers that is different from (better than) our competition?

Along with leaders defining the segment potential, an early evaluation of the "customer's choice potential" should be accomplished. The company needs to know this in order to realistically move forward with its development programs. This early understanding allows teams to better plan for the feasibility of the product. The QFD process will support making this decision by balancing between the customers "choice" priorities and their perceptions of the competition.

What measures and target values are used by my customers to know that we are supplying them with products that provide what they want?

The identification of the values the customer uses to define a favorable result is the next important consideration. The CIDM/QFD process develops an in-context view, through interviews and observation, of the problems the customer is encountering in attaining the result they need.

CIDM uses "analysis ladders" (discussed in part III) and advanced methods like "controlled experiments" to understand the customers' measures of delight and satisfaction. These "experiments" are much like the design of experiments that technical engineers use to make design decisions, only they are used to understand the "choice" processes regarding functions and feature combinations and the effects of price on decision-making.

What level of importance do we give these measures and target values as they apply to the customers' "choice"-making processes?

The CIDM/QFD process utilizes "choice"- and "satisfaction"-based evaluations of the importance perceptions of the potential user of our product. Referring back to our discussion on the dimensions of quality, we will work to discover those attributes that will provide a desire to buy—the structure of quality—as well as those things that will satisfy the customer—the functions of quality.

A baseline tool, the $100 and $1,000 test, is explained in detail in chapter 9. What we are interested in is understanding the customer's potential for purchasing our solution. We use this simple tool to ask the question: Where would you spend money to get what you want? This survey approach contrasts with "satisfaction" questions that ask, "On a scale" what is important? Or What are you not happy with? The differences are important—customers often buy what doesn't make them happy because of the relative value of the overall solution to their "choice-making" process. One, preferred, approach is the "choice prediction models," called "single unit market models," supplied by Eric Marder Associates. Using these and QFD matrices, we can discover the way customers segment themselves. It's a fallacy that companies segment customers—customers group themselves. Companies can influence this grouping but have to know the benefit that's wanted first.

What is the perceived value of our product in relation to its price?

The answer to this question is most often not understood by companies. We must evaluate, from the perceptions of the "customers," what the "value" of "benefit for price" is for our solution.

We cannot fail to understand, as well as we can, how this issue is perceived. Unfortunately, we most often get into price wars— competition for "feature/function" versus price—and forget the notion of "value." We need to know what benefit we are providing for the price we charge.

How does the customer view our product's capabilities and perceive our competition's capabilities?

Here, we are faced with the task of understanding, from the perception of the customer—not our own "feelings" what the capabilities of our solution are compared with the options customers have. These options are not always other providers of solutions in our industry but also providers outside our industry.

What attributes and/or combination of attributes affect customers' "choice-based" decision-making? And how do we predict their reactions before we develop our solution?

One of the challenges we have as solution providers is making decisions on the combinations of features, functions, and price in developing our solution definitions. This effort must be done, to be effective, from the point of view of the "choice" perceptions of our "customers." Here, again, the company must make decisions and simple tools like $100/$1,000 tests will help. Processes like single unit market models are able to predict quantitatively, with high accuracy and validity, how much the customer will value our "definition of requirements."

Do you understand the answers to these questions from the customer's perspective and perception?

The important awareness is that *our* impression of the value of our products and our customers' perception of the value of our products are most often different. If there is a difference on the negative side—we think our product is more valuable than our customers do—regarding significant "choice importance," then there will be a major market performance shortfall.

Companies must understand this across all of the "value delivery process"—marketing, engineering, manufacturing, distribution, and service.

"Value Delivery Differentiation"

Author Bill Barnard found this customer understanding approach in a paper he received from the Daihen Corporation in 1988—they are a Japanese maker of welding and power products. This paper described their use of QFD in product development. The actual description of this concept of data acquisitions is as follows:

> After the fields of application for the new product were defined, our salespeople and development engineers personally gathered information by "getting to the real site" (GENCHI), taking a look at the "real matter" (GEMBUTSU) and "listening to what the real customer, or field operator, would have to say" (GEMBA) about the product to identify the true needs of the customers. We called this the "three real survey," (Three-GEN). It has proved to be quite effective in collecting fresh information as to what bothers the customers and what they want."

The essence of this approach was also practiced at Hewlett-Packard and is now a major part of the CIDM/QFD approach as in-context market research and in-context customer visits. It is through this approach that we will find definitions of value.

In part III, we will define how the components of the QFD/CIDM affect results in more detail. The following is a discussion about a concept that provides the context for our reference to an overall solution we call the BIG P. It describes the idea of a "valuable solution" as being one that has a high degree of understanding regarding structural quality, i.e., all of the contributions a company makes in providing a "value delivery differentiation." See figure 3.6.

Figure 3.6

Understanding the "Value Delivery Proposition"

Knowing:

The customers' perception of: Value = $\dfrac{\text{Marketing-Engineering-Manufacturing-Distribution-Service Benefits}}{\text{Price}}$

Our company's competencies and decisions that create: Value = $\dfrac{\text{Marketing-Engineering-Manufacturing-Distribution-Service Benefits}}{\text{Price}}$

Our understanding of the competition's ability to provide: Value = $\dfrac{\text{Marketing-Engineering-Manufacturing-Distribution-Service Benefits}}{\text{Price}}$

Shown graphically, defining a superior "value delivery proposition" is supported by being able to identify the differentiations among the many *Little p* components.

What the company then can do is better understand the "differentiation" opportunities within which they can compete profitably.

An often asked question about CIDM is what results can I expect and when? The following pages will expand on the discussion from part I by describing a time line for results expectations and sequence of introducing actions to cause these results. The "expectations ladder" will describe the benefits to be expected by phase. We describe four results phases; from the fastest results to expect, through the results that will take the longest to realize. The overall results are those that occur eventually, some sooner than others, and in fact more accurately reflect the goals of the efforts of a company in doing business. For purposes of this book, we have attempted to define a "time parameter" for each. Reality, however, is that individual companies will realize results differently based on the effort and intensity placed on succeeding.

The "Expectations Ladder"

BENEFIT EXPECTATIONS

The end results after a focused and conscious effort for two or three years will be the total evolution to "lower market misses for our solution decisions" and the monetary results desired. It is important that in the beginning, companies see the canceling of projects that will not be profitable and the redefining of strategies for markets in which to compete as some of the "results." Interestingly enough, the company moves as Bill BonDurant, former marketing research director for Hewlett-Packard, used to say, "Simulating its failures and marketing its successes."

Overall results
  Higher sales
  Reduced time to market
  Lower percentage of market misses
  Lower warranty costs
  Improved company image

Phase 1 Results

These results occur almost immediately. The fact that the team works together to understand the customer will cause the improvement in "data visibility" and the "reduction of functional silos." The structured approach that CIDM supports coupled with direct customer contact will provide immediate results.

More customer focus

More complete and more visible data regarding customer needs, competitive information—from the customer's perspective, and team decision information

Breaking down of functional silos in the multifunctionality and/or multinationality of the company

Better cross-functional communication

Better team understanding of the customer

More of a consensus decision-making environment

Phase 2 Results

Higher percentage of employees skilled in market research and the means to understand customers

Higher percentage of employees skilled in analyzing customer research data

Improved rationality of decision-making for solution development

Customer data more accessible to more of the company

Stability of solution specifications

Fewer engineering changes

Shorter design time

Reduced project cycle

Lower project costs

Phase 3 Results

Improved company reputation for exerting the effort to understand the customer

Increased willingness of customers to share ideas for needs

In developing a "learning organization," the continued use of the CIDM methodology is important. The teams will develop a "market-focused" environment and begin to require more education on market research processes. Ultimately, the company will see the need to develop ways of communicating the research results and a way to store and retrieve this data—manual at first, then automated approaches should be planned. The net result will be an improvement of processes and therefore shorter times to make decisions and the resulting cost and cycle time reductions.

ACTIONS INVOLVED BY PHASE

The following list defines the actions that we see companies pursuing and the approximate phase they do, gaining the most results. These actions provide the results discussed in part I's previous list of expectations.

We see teams most often gaining the most value by moving away from a political internal environment, toward an external customer environment. This simple action develops an environment that allows individuals, involved in politically focused "work groups," to move toward becoming real "teams," in the words of Rick Norman, "high-energy adaptive teams" (HEATs). This environment is nurtured—in fact, allowed to happen—through the use of QFD.

Phase 1

Strategic and Tactical—Internal—Intangible

Action—Multifunctional teaming

Action—In-context customer visits and "choice decision" understanding

Action—The use of QFD

The next phase of actions is to continue the process of QFD by linking decisions made in Phase I CIDM/QFD efforts to decision-making for parts and processes. There are many ways that teams can continue a solution realization effort, but without a linking and formalization, like that provided by the continued use of QFD tools, it seems that teams lose the knowledge they acquire in the first phase of the CIDM/QFD effort. We know of many tools that teams can use—concurrent engineering, design of experiments, TRIZ, etc.—but they all require that the original decisions made are from the customer viewpoint. So far, no other "front-end" process does as well as CIDM/QFD in adequately answering the question: What does the customer want?

Through the continued use of CIDM/QFD, leaders will begin to gain confidence in the teams' ability to "know the right answer," and if they listen, leaders will realize they can also learn things they don't know from the team. This "bidirectional empowerment" from the CIDM/QFD process learning will fuel further confidence in each other.

Phase 2

Strategic and Tactical—Internal—Tangible

> Action—Bidirectional empowerment through continued use of Phase 1 methods

> Action—Use of the "QFD matrices" for linked phase decision-making

The next step we see is the ability of teams to be able to work in a "proactive" method with customers. This comes about through their improved understanding of customer problems and the multifunctional teaming to solve it. The continued use of in-context customer visits supports this result, the teams become better at researching and probing the customer, and the result is they become better at providing solutions.

Strategic and Tactical—Marketplace—Intangible

> Action—Continued use of the in-context visit program to include providing proactive solutions to the customer

The last effort we see, although it should happen as soon as possible, is the internalization of the CIDM/QFD process. This is accomplished by integrating CIDM/QFD with the company's other business processes. The problem, most often, is the lack of business processes such as formal product definition and development methods. This final effort is the most important. It also must link to the other business processes to gain value for the company.

Phase 3

Strategic and Tactical—Tangible

    Action—Internalize the CIDM/QFD process

Baseline Activity List

A brief activity list follows. It outlines the basic high-level activities that a team will need to accomplish in completing a CIDM/QFD project. The list in Appendix VIII indicates the average number of workdays the team can expect to commit to.

PHASE 1: PRODUCT CHARACTERISTIC DEVELOPMENT

Objective: Development of benefit characteristics and measurements

Steps

    Acquire—In-context customer data

    Reduce—The data acquired—wants/needs

    Develop—The measures for the wants/needs

    Develop—Come to consensus on the relationship

    Acquire—"Choice" importance and competitive perception data

    Estimated Time: 53 working days

PHASE 2—STRATEGY DEPLOYMENT

    Estimated Time: ongoing

PHASE 3—CHARACTERISTIC DEPLOYMENT

Objective: Identification of key part characteristics, and selection of new or best design concepts

Steps

Transfer—Priority measures from HOQ to action matrix

Complete—Function chart "voice of the developer"

Identify—All action attributes—construct affinity/tree diagrams

Identify—Degree of importance of action options—rank

Transfer—All "voice of company" requirements from HOQ

Complete—Relationship matrix

Calculate—Importance weight of technical requirements

Analyze—Action matrix

Identify—Action concepts

Complete—Concept selection

Identify—Target values of parts and features of current product

Analyze—Product design matrix

Estimated Time: 16 working days

Summary

As you begin to use CIDM/QFD in your organization, these benefits and timelines will become more real. It is hoped that at this stage of your learning, you will start to get some understanding of the breadth and scope, as well as the potential, of the process.

CHAPTER 4

Making CIDM/QFD Work in Your Company

Getting value from CIDM/QFD requires an understanding of the mind-set in creating an environment for success. Results come from an integration of processes, but more importantly from the realization that success comes to companies following the guidelines in figure 4.1.

Figure 4.1

Success Results from CIDM/QFD

Because the company does the:

- Right research on the right customers.
- Right decision-making with the right team.
- Right action deployment.

Understanding How CIDM/QFD Contributes to Success

THE PROBLEM WITH "READY, FIRE, AIM"

In the article "Japan's Dark Side of Time," in the July/August 1993 *Harvard Business Review,* George Stalk revisits his 1988 article in the same journal, "Time—The Next Source of Competition," and discusses the issues of implementation that have arisen. As we have interpreted his words regarding the "time-based competition gone mad," there is a flaw in simply introducing products into the market fast. In fact, there is a criticism of even introducing "innovative" products into the markets fast.

The most important description of "value adding time-based competition" is described on page 101 of that same article by Stalk as "third stage time-based competition:"

"Companies alter their momentum. They stop simply doing everything faster and put speed and innovation to work in the service of the customer. [They] build the skills of their employees to create competitive advantage."

The key to stage three is focus:

"[They] bear an integrated system that focuses on understanding the needs of customers and the capabilities of competitors, segmenting customers by their sensitivity to time, prioritizing improvement efforts within the company. . . .

"Management must . . . create identifiable and exploitable competitive advantage."

This is what CIDM/QFD is about. Over sixty experiences as a total CIDM project and one hundred projects utilizing most of the methods in a project prove the ability to support companies as they move to "customer integrated."

CIDM/QFD is an enriched process that provides practical methods to support four broad phases described in figure 4.2.

Figure 4.2

Four Phases of CIDM/QFD

- Market identification
- Idea generation
- Idea test
- Action deployment

Simply described, CIDM phases integrate Stalk's stage one cycle time—putting products into the market faster (with some sobering failures)—and stage two cycle time—putting "innovative" products (usually technical in nature and often unlinked to customer needs and wants, often also with less than desirable profit results)—with more customer-integrated methods to develop a stage three cycle-time culture.

Bob Frankenberg, now CEO of Novell, formerly VP and general manager of Hewlett-Packard's Personal Information Products Group (PCs, computing servers, and networks), used the following analogies when talking about this strong profit contributing group at HP. He described the successful introduction of a four-computer-products family in six months' total cycle time. To achieve this, he defined the following requirements:

Effectiveness—do the right things.
Efficiency—Do things right.

CIDM supports this approach by integrating tool sets and methodologies that allow a company to accomplish "Ready, aim, fire," instead of "Fire, fix, fire," etc.

READY—IDENTIFYING THE "RIGHT THINGS"

Define the correct mission, scope, and objectives.

Identify the profit segment, or make sure we understand we are working in an investment segment.

Identify the right customer viewpoints to research.

AIM—UNDERSTANDING THE "RIGHT THINGS"

Using in-context and "choice-based" processes, acquire the right knowledge of the wants and needs of the customers.

Identify the right "characteristics and measures" used by the customer to know we are meeting their wants and needs.

Set the right priorities for those "characteristics."

Make all of our decisions with regard to an internalized understanding of the competition's ability to provide for these "characteristics" of a solution for the customer's "wants and needs."

FIRE—DOING THE "RIGHT THINGS RIGHT"

Take action on these prioritized "characteristics," using understandings benchmarked against the customer's definition of
the "target values" that represent delight and/or satisfaction—
not against our definition or our competition's abilities.

Use an interactive "catchball" process to deploy these potential
breakthroughs throughout the company. Do not rely on "management by objective" approaches that limit the potential for
success by overwhelming individual contributors by "launching them armed for failure."

Options for Integrating CIDM/QFD with Other Processes

The notion of defining integrated processes to develop "value delivery differentiated" solutions is described within CIDM. Integrated
programs like it are used by companies like Hewlett-Packard and
Procter & Gamble to achieve success in the marketplace. In this
section, we will describe the differences between CIDM—a complete "program"-oriented process—and using QFD alone—a more
"product or action" development process.

Figures 4.3–4.8 graphically demonstrate these differences and
the support each provides.

SOLUTION REALIZATION PROCESS (SRP)

A solution realization process is a comprehensive integration of
processes to define objectives and develop action recommendations and priorities. This approach requires that there be structure
and an environmental potential for accomplishment. Each of the

process components must be simple and provisions made for education and training. The company must define the results expected and the measurement to be used to describe success.

The use of CIDM as a core-enabling process will assure in this SRP that the objectives, expectations, priorities, and actions are all linked to the final customers' measurements of success.

A subset of this SRP is often referred to as the "product development process" and many times considered a stand-alone process. CIDM requires this subset process to be defined and structured. Historically, QFD got its start here, as a tool for engineers, a tool to link marketing and engineering. Most often, QFD is used in a

Figure 4.3

Solution Realization Process

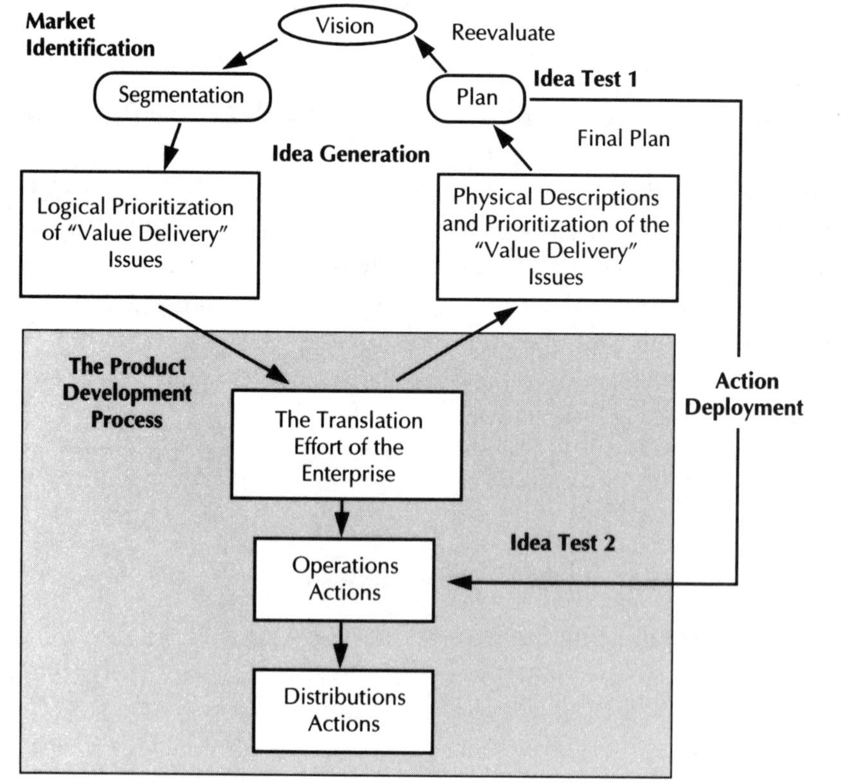

Figure 4.4

Product Development Process

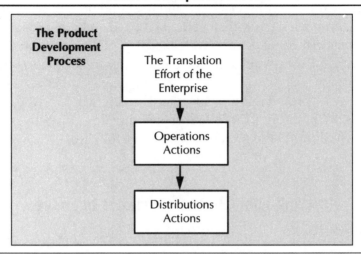

product development effort by engineering teams to make decisions that are "customer focused." CIDM utilizes QFD at the strategy and the product level to assure a consciously more valuable solution. It supports both *Little p* and BIG P, as well as strategic decision-making.

More specifically, the impact of integrated approaches (mind-set) compared with stand-alone (tool set) approaches on the achievement of goals can be analyzed as follows.

The objectives of utilizing Customer-Integrated Decision-Making are listed in figure 4.5.

Figure 4.5

CIDM Objectives

- Provide the ability to acquire and retain a clear understanding of the enterprise mission and charter.
- Assure an adequate flow of successful products.
- Achieve targeted product shipments.
- Achieve or exceed targeted profit.

The objectives seem simple, but getting results requires the company to accept this "structured" way of doing things. The problem most often is that the first objective is not done well, which causes the company to misapply resources and to spend time in conflict. The CIDM approach starts with developing a solid multifunctional agreement on the mission, scope, and objectives of the project. More importantly, CIDM requires the team to confront decisions to change that mission based on customer-balanced data. Sometimes the team finds out the project is the wrong one. This discovery and the change of mission will work to accomplish the other three objectives just as well as finding out the project should move forward.

Assuring That CIDM Contributes to Success

QFD-based CIDM components contribute to realizing these goals as follows:

Figure 4.6

CIDM Contributions

S=Strong Contribution, M=Medium Contribution, W=Weak Contribution

	CIDM		
	Market Research (Choice)	QFD	Strategy Deployment
Provide the ability to acquire and retain a clear understanding of the enterprise mission and charter	M	M	S
Assure an adequate flow of successful products	S	M	M
Achieve targeted product shipments	n/a	S	M
Achieve or exceed targeted profit	M	S	M

CIDM's and QFD's integration with other "interventions" can be evaluated in figure 4.7.

Figure 4.7

CIDM Integration with a "Solution Realization Process" Mind-set Approach

S=Strong Contribution, M=Medium Contribution, W=Weak Contribution

	MIND-SET APPROACH CIDM						
	Business Planning Processes	Phased Review Processes	Market Research (Choice)	QFD	Strategy Deployment	MRP Production Planning	Cost Control Practices
Provide the ability to acquire and retain a clear understanding of the enterprise mission and charter	S	M	M	M	S	n/a	n/a
Assure an adequate flow of successful products	S	S	S	M	M	n/a	W
Achieve targeted product shipments	W	M	n/a	S	M	S	W
Achieve or exceed targeted profit	M	W	M	S	M	M	S

75

THE "TOOL SET" APPROACH

Figure 4.8

QFD as Product Development Tool Set

S=Strong Contribution, M=Medium Contribution, W=Weak Contribution

	TOOL SET APPROACH QFD
Provide the ability to acquire and retain a clear understanding of the enterprise mission and charter	M
Assure an adequate flow of successful products	M
Achieve targeted product shipments	M
Achieve or exceed targeted profit	W

PROCESS APPROACHES REVIEWED

In part I, we talked about how QFD is executed. The discussion focused around describing a rigorous approach and a four-phased approach. A more important discussion is one that focuses on the use of the approaches in relation to the "mission, scope, and objective" to be accomplished.

The issue of execution is usually one that discusses the use of either a "four-phased model"—the phased definition of product characteristics, part characteristics, process characteristics, and process control characteristics, or a "robust matrix of matrices" approach—utilizing many matrices to answer questions regarding quality, function, cost, and reliability. CIDM/QFD's view is that the problem is one of understanding and defining the project's objectives and then defining the "road map" that is necessary to accomplish the results required in defining the solution.

More importantly is the completeness of the efforts to acquire customer data.

CIDM adds the important steps of "market identification"—segmentation, customer identification, team identification—all supported by customer-integrated project management. The next step is the use of in-context customer visits during the "idea generation" step and the observational and interviewing processes it provides. This is coupled with understanding importance based on either or both "choice" and "satisfaction" to improve the value of the QFD decisions.

The actions of data analyses that involve QFD will be highly enriched, and the use of the QFD matrix tools will be defined by the objectives of the study. The CIDM processes utilize the four phases in figure 4.5 to better differentiate the project management effort and allow for as many QFD matrices as required in each of those phases.

The idea that there are a specific number of charts that must be completed is not required by CIDM. Rather, CIDM focuses on the belief in the value of the matrix analysis tool. Teaching the use of this tool to teams improves the teaming process; this improves the decision-making process, which improves the final results. The definition of what is needed comes from a team that works better together, and they define the decision matrices that are required. The need to define phases of the QFD effort is that of doing a good job of project management.

Bill Kern, of Integrated Project Systems, in Belmont, California, and Bill Barnard have created a CIDM/QFD and project management approach called Customer-Integrated Project Management, which utilizes CIDM to define objectives. The phases of definition most useful are to understand the product (or solution) characteristics, and then the part (or method) characteristic, etc. The number and type of matrices are best defined by a team focused on the specific outcome needs of the project.

CHAPTER 5

Establishing the Infrastructure

Future Quality

CIDM/QFD integrates and supports the strategic dimensions of quality and integrates them with the other dimensions of quality, choice (structure), and function. In doing this, CIDM creates a quality dimension we call future quality. This quality dimension supports leaders in making decisions through *adaptive leadership*.

The essential components of this process are:

- Multifunctional and/or multicultural teaming efforts to acquire customer knowledge.
- Matrix formatted information and knowledge archiving.
- Structured retrieving of the customer's knowledge while team decisions are made, while recombining this knowledge with the company's technical competencies.

The major action steps that the process involves are shown in Figure 5.1:

Figure 5.1

Future Quality

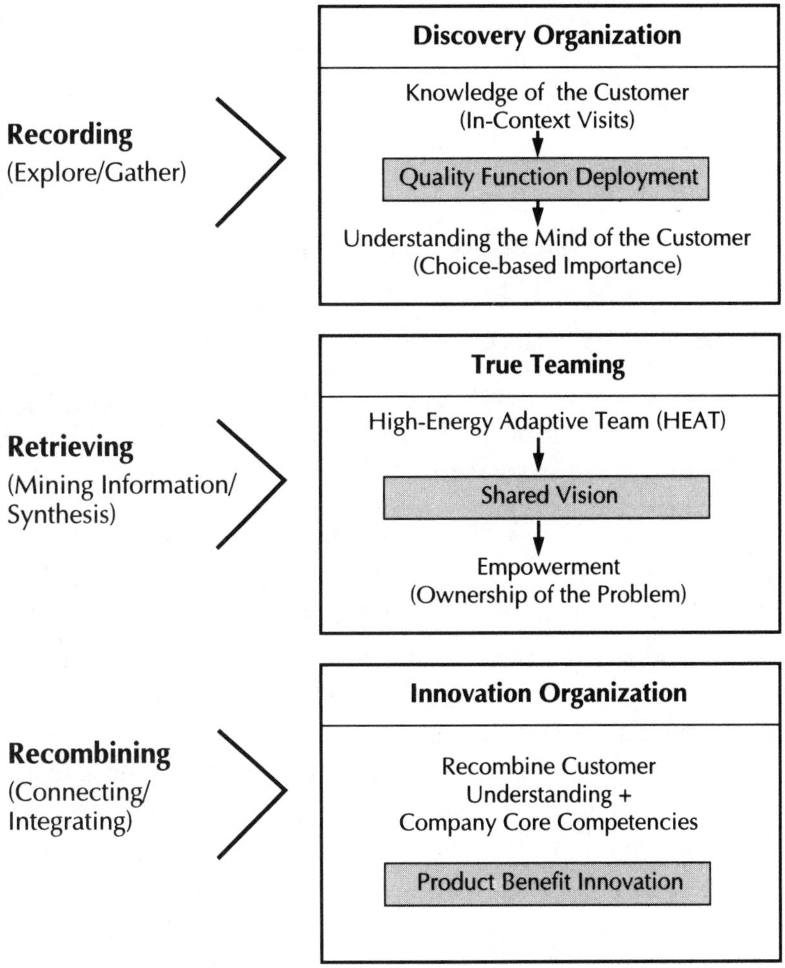

Recording
(Explore/Gather)

> **Discovery Organization**
>
> Knowledge of the Customer
> (In-Context Visits)
> ↓
> Quality Function Deployment
> ↓
> Understanding the Mind of the Customer
> (Choice-based Importance)

Retrieving
(Mining Information/
Synthesis)

> **True Teaming**
>
> High-Energy Adaptive Team (HEAT)
> ↓
> Shared Vision
> ↓
> Empowerment
> (Ownership of the Problem)

Recombining
(Connecting/
Integrating)

> **Innovation Organization**
>
> Recombine Customer
> Understanding +
> Company Core Competencies
>
> Product Benefit Innovation

This approach will produce and define innovation and when coupled with "tested competitive pricing" will be seen by the customer as differentiated value.

The CIDM approach uses QFD to support multifunctional teams as they translate "customer knowledge." This is accomplished utilizing QFD's "matrix" analysis approach. In the past, we have tried to translate "satisfaction surveys" into action. In the "future quality" paradigm, we translate knowledge of the customer's "choice-making" processes into "value delivery" action.

This provides a multifunctional team, with an integrated "value delivery" view and gives them the knowledge to accept "responsibility for the ownership" of developing a solution.

Details on Future Quality

THE DISCOVERY ORGANIZATION

This set of activities develops a complete "understanding" of the customer, utilizing tools that focus on "hands-on" data-gathering efforts—in-context market research and "choice"-based customer market research.

TEAMING

Teaming is developed and realized as a by-product of using structured processes like QFD. The CIDM/QFD approach provides support during data acquisition and decision-making.

A main point contributing to success is that the team must be multifunctional, must contain a "viewpoint" from all value-contributing solution providers in the organization. Working together provides both a horizontally and vertically integrated result.

THE INNOVATION ORGANIZATION

"Innovation" is an often discussed, yet still obscure, term that we think has differing perspectives:

"Innovation" historically seems to imply "advanced technology."
"Innovation" in the eyes of the "choice" maker, however, may be very different.

"Innovation" in practice often seems to be the "delight" about the innovative methods used by the supplier to understand and "deliver" a solution. This may be as simple as "a solution that does what it says it will do." Many innovations occur by the focused combination of customer needs and our core competencies.

Adaptive Leadership

What we want to introduce is an environment for more "adaptive leadership." Much has been written regarding "managing chaos"—but experience has shown that identifying chaos, much less managing it, is not realistic.

An alternative strategy is to develop an organization that has high flexibility in adapting to market and customer change. This organization, in place in some companies today—Hewlett-Packard versus competitors such as IBM and DEC—will have a flexible teaming atmosphere. This environment will work well both horizontally and vertically and will be able to internalize data acquired and turn it into knowledge faster, and with a higher quality.

Adaptive leadership is the fourth quality dimension—that of knowing how to flexibly gain focused knowledge rapidly, and then translate it clearly and accurately. The target is a fourth quality dimension—that of adaptive leadership or future quality.

Gaining Acceptance of CIDM/QFD

THE ISSUES AND THE LIMITERS

In trying to anticipate the issues that will need to be understood to overcome objections to this new approach, it is useful to examine the drivers that define the need. That is, why in the global competitive market there is an increasing need for customer-integrated approaches.

The company team members state that there has not been a problem in the past with competition and that the issue they face today is price-based.

The reply to this is to discuss the following:

COMPETITION

One key driver is competition. In a world of global markets and dizzying amounts of information, we are faced with the fact that customers have more choice now than ever before. The result is a more sophisticated and prudent buyer—therefore, the very nature of competition is changing rapidly. Another issue is that competitors are collaborating (Apple and IBM, for example) in areas not imagined just a few years ago. Thus, we are competing for customers' dollars in more complex and less definable ways.

Some examples of the dilemma are:

- *Cross-product:* A customer may decide to buy equipment for a home office rather than a new car for work.
- *Cross-industry:* A customer may decide to hold off buying a new VCR because a new interactive TV device is a better choice for accessing movie options.
- *Temporal:* Higher-quality products are lasting longer. Our own new products may cannibalize our existing line. Competitors are able to get products out faster than we can.

The very nature of competing requires deeper and broader understanding of our environment. Indeed, those who were once your competitors are now allies; and those who once made no difference are taking our market share.

We need new tools to be able to accomplish new objectives—some of the most important tools are segmentation, customer identification. We need to use these tools more often and comprehensively in our decision-making process.

VOICE OF THE CUSTOMER

Because of an increasingly complex competitive environment, a more comprehensive understanding of customers is critical. People buy products to satisfy a need or to provide a benefit. People don't always describe the best solution, only the need they "know about." People change their minds, or are influenced to, in a competitive environment. Understanding takes time.

Understanding comes through paying attention to details and realizing their interactions. The voice of the customer must now become a continuous process. What are the trends? What are the fundamental needs? How is change being affected?

The need for more in-context contact with the customer exists— we need to observe as well as listen. We need to match our research efforts to the correct customer. We need to be influenced by understanding "choice" decision-making more or in combination with satisfaction understanding.

Jesse Peterson, a manager at the Ritz-Carlton Hotel in Detroit, Michigan, overheard Bill Barnard comment about a need to make his stay more comfortable. Jesse overheard this as he walked ahead of Barnard in a hallway in the hotel. Doing so, he turned and stopped Barnard, asked his room number, and assured him that he would take care of the need. The need, humidifying an air-conditioned room, was beyond the perfect service and room offering at the Ritz. To Jesse, his "in-context" contact with Barnard gave him an opportunity to provide the "delight" factor to make a room even more comfortable. Jesse made sure it was done. The Ritz is a Baldrige award winner—it's not hard to see why with managers like Jesse.

REACTION TIME

In a world of increasing and variable competition, our ability to respond quickly to changing needs and market shifts becomes more important. Time-to-market becomes more of an issue of time-to-sale, by providing solutions from a more accurate understanding of value "differentiation." In the complex process of product realization, we can react faster if we know—with a high degree of predictability—

what the customers want and what our competencies are. We must recombine customer benefit understanding with our core competencies to provide innovation in value delivery.

CIDM/QFD works to develop a confidence and a sense of commitment by involving the whole company team in understanding and consenting to the solution. This reduces time to reach agreement and the wasted politics often associated with "blind technology solution"–driven events.

PREDICTION

We must be able to predict more accurately what the customers will buy and when, and then be able to react quickly and more accurately.

An effort to understand complexity and chaos says that we can't predict a chaotic system's immediate behavior, but that order emerges in a chaotic system over time. Conversely, information overload creates chaos in human systems. We propose that in many companies, the product development processes in effect are so disintegrated that they themselves cause information overload.

CIDM/QFD supports author Bill Barnard's first rule of "integrated solution"—"You can't solve an integrated problem with a disintegrated solution"—and works to provide an integrated structure and method to a complex environment. Understanding trends implies observing data over time: We will seek to acquire data and analyze their interactions, and in doing so find order in the voice of the customer and track our competitors' strategies. By having and analyzing customer data quickly and efficiently, we can become more predictive.

Another "wall" the company might try to throw up is a discussion on why there needs to be a "formal" process, why isn't the way we have done it all along good enough?

A reply to those questions will focus on the following.

DISCIPLINE

The *American Heritage Dictionary* defines discipline as: "Training expected to produce a specific character or pattern of behavior, especially training that produces . . . mental improvement." It goes on to state that when used as a verb, the meaning is "to impose order on."

CIDM/QFD is a discipline for product development. It is "doing" product development conceptually. CIDM/QFD is structured and practical "market identification and idea generation." To paraphrase Bill BonDurant, the former director of the Market Research Information Center for Hewlett-Packard, now at Xerox, "We seek to simulate our failures and to be able to better market our successes."

We move away from refining our products in the market after the customer complains and we have to. CIDM/QFD should be viewed as a never-ending "refinement" of the product "proactively." This is the discipline of CIDM/QFD.

ORGANIZATIONAL LEARNING

An organizational intervention many organizations are now embracing is the concept of a "learning organization." Peter Senge has defined it as a new way of organizational thinking that comes about from practicing disciplines he calls systems thinking, personal mastery, team learning, mental models, and shared vision.

Its essence is understanding how the interconnectedness of things determines its behavior. How choices we make about structure create our future, how synergy of thought and action by teams emerge through dialogue, how bureaucratic barriers to progress can be overcome by raising and testing our fundamental assumptions. More importantly, how creating a common view of the future can energize teaming activity.

CIDM/QFD provides the structure and the mechanisms to create an environment conducive to internalizing "organizational knowledge."

The next "limiter" to success that skeptics often will bring up will have to do with cycle time and the need to get to market faster. Along with our discussion of "cycle time" in chapter 4, the following discussion on concept development needs to be emphasized.

We have found that CIDM/QFD's ability to better define concepts early, with more rigor and focus, enhances our capability to make decisions faster in subsequent phases.

CONCEPT DEVELOPMENT

One of the most important steps that is most often not attempted in a formal structure is the "idea generation" step and the downstream step of concept selection. To revisit the process of solution development, the following outline shows where concept selection fits.

Figure 5.2

Concept Development

The "Management Product"

- Management Objectives Defined

Market Identification

- Segments
- Customers

Idea Generation

- In-Context Customer Visits
- QFD:
  - Need/Want Identification
  - Solution Characteristic Identification
  - Characteristic Prioritization
  - Other phases to define cause & effect relationships for parts, processes, process control
  - Customer "Choice" understanding
  - Concept Selection

Idea Test

- Customer "Choice" prediction related to the characteristics of our solution

- Concept Selection

- Controlled Marketing Experiments on "feature/function" options for our solution

The challenge is to formalize all of these steps into a rapidly executable process and internalize it in the company. CIDM/QFD practitioners will be more successful in doing so due to the practical and replicatable nature of this process.

The image resulting from the work done to build a QFD "house" we often compare to that of a "paper prototype." In completing this matrix, or any of the submatrices, the result is support for creating an explicit concept—a skeleton built upon highly structured data. A visualization of the "real" thing, then, can be exercised mentally and figuratively so that decisions can be made about the concept's fundamental architecture.

To be able to maintain thought at a conceptual level and experiment broadly at the next level in order to understand the meaning of potential competitiveness is an art and a discipline that few teams with which we have worked possess.

CIDM/QFD is a tool set that supports strategy evolution. As it becomes more of a mind-set, it will be the process from which profitable products emerge quickly. It is scenario planning taken into the realm of product development. CIDM/QFD provides the underlying structure and principles for developing robust explicit concepts.

COMMUNICATION

A picture is worth a thousand words. CIDM/QFD charts create a lexicon of symbols that have meaning. As the charts are constructed by a team, visual representations of decisions emerge. These data create images in the mind. A trail emerges from literally thousands of data items. These logic flows are tested once they are thought out and then displayed in a visual form that "binds" discussion and limits emotion and political decision-making.

Realizing which definitions of "wants, needs, and characteristics" vary over time, which remain fuzzy, and which are measurable makes the process of product trade-off decision-making much more meaningful. An important understanding is that these matrices are full of words that may have many meanings in the context of multifunctional teams. The CIDM structure guides the team through definition and consensus gaining "team" meaning of these words. The nature of CIDM/QFD supports the power of visual communication.

SCRUBBING THE COMPANIES' FINGERTIPS

In our daily lives, we are literally overwhelmed with the volume of information we must deal with. The question becomes: "What information do we need to make better decisions?" CIDM/QFD provides the structure and architecture for development teams to understand *what* information is important. Competitive companies of the future will be able to acquire and process information faster than competitors, therefore making better decisions faster, and with a higher degree of confidence.

Some of the strongest objectors will be the "lone wolves" that will question the need for "teaming" and why it's now being stressed.

We need to "team" for the following reasons.

RELATIONSHIPS

How do we understand risk? How do we embrace uncertainty? How do we understand the complexities of our situation? CIDM/QFD presents a structure that models reality in the solution realization process. CIDM begins the understanding of the relationships that exist between the customer-demanded quality and the measurable parameters that we must deal with to deliver it.

By understanding those relationships, our actions become more definitive and certain. Our efficiencies are improved because our effectiveness in the marketplace is obvious. The essence of CIDM is about identifying and bringing all the variables affecting us under control.

CIDM/QFD is about putting the product realization structure in perspective prior to developing the product.

Preparing the Infrastructure

"ANALOG" VERSUS "BINARY CHANGE"

It is important to approach the CIDM effort with the correct expectations. It is even more important to approach the effort with an understanding of how realistic the expectations for change are. The results will often occur faster than the change that must sustain it on a continuing basis. Therefore, management must constantly remind itself, as well as work to overcome the frustrations of the team attempting the process introduction, that there will not be a "binary" or immediate change as a result of the project. The change in the culture and the change in the process will take time—it will appear more like an "analog" change. The results will occur from the project, but for the culture to internalize the process and be able to "replicate it" again and again, the company must be prepared to experience and understand the process well enough to make the internal changes structurally and psychologically that are required. A couple of the CIDM/QFD practitioners at Motorola Land Mobile Products Sector have done a great job of documenting the issues they saw as they and Bill Barnard worked to "change" the culture and internalize the process. One of the primary reasons they saw was summarized in this passage: "Why do some QFD projects succeed and others fail? We began to believe that 'succeeding' or 'failing' was not caused by the QFD process. We began to speculate that the results of a QFD project were more directly attributed to the environment into which QFD was being introduced."

The report they presented at the "Sixth Symposium on Quality Function Deployment—1994"[1] goes on to list four roles that must exist in an environment to assure process change. There must be:

1. "Sponsors"—those who give the team time, dollars, etc.
2. "Agents"—those who make the change happen.
3. "Targets"—the group who must accomplish the change (all members of the team and management).

4. "Advocates"—those who want change to happen but lack the power to make it happen (a training director or quality director).

The management team must therefore be prepared to utilize all of the powers it has to "hold on" during the transition period.

We believe that "organizational patience" is a term that the company should use as a motto along with "total quality" and "voice of the customer." Organizational patience refers to the understanding by all top, middle, and individual contributors—it refers to the compassion and understanding that each should have for the other during this transition time. The intent is that the team will work as hard as it can to successfully internalize the CIDM/QFD process but that management will remember that it not only wants the results of understanding the customer better for the first project, but that it also wants to begin a transition from the past "technology driven" approach to a more customer-balanced culture.

Scott Berkey, vice president from CINCOM Systems, and John Edholm, vice president from Pierce and Stevens, are two such managers—they constantly repeat to the team this simple support statement: "We want the results, but more importantly we want change." Then they spend time in the trenches listening and understanding their teams—supporting them positively, and leading them to success.

THE FIRST PILOT PROJECT

Much has been said about the way to approach introducing change in a company, and like many other things, there seems to be a balance on which approach is best. The bottom line for CIDM/QFD is that it works best when introduced slowly and with successes providing the foundation for future successes. Authors Barnard and Daetz were a major part of the introduction of QFD at Hewlett-Packard and very much involved at Motorola. Author Barnard was responsible for the CIDM/QFD effort at ATT/NCR. The learning from these efforts is that "mass" training of the whole company does not work as well as individually supported introductions. We call this "just-in-time" training, and it is supported by a pilot-based internalization.

JUST-IN-TIME TRAINING FOR THE "TEAM" AND THE "FACILITATOR"

In JIT training, the team and internal facilitator are supported by an experienced "practitioner." This person may have to come from outside the company initially. There are many options here, ranging from other companies you partner with and trust to a few providers with experienced facilitators that can be used for a specific period to perform the support efforts required. The final result desired is that you will have provided an internal facilitator the opportunity to be trained and successfully complete a project and then become the only facilitator. Hewlett-Packard had a QFD facilitator group, often reaching ninety people worldwide, that met at least twice a year to discuss issues regarding QFD's use in the company. ATT/NCR had a group that met at least once a year to discuss issues regarding QFD and marketing research. All of these efforts promoted the movement from technology-driven to market-balanced cultures.

The objective is to promote the change by assuring success in the first projects. Once success begins to occur, it might take a couple of efforts and the measurement of success will not always be the same one in subsequent projects; then the culture will begin to change itself. Mass trainings fall short in that often by the time the individuals start to use the skills presented, they have forgotten the important nuances of the process. The issue also is that without an experienced practitioner, the team will have to make its own discoveries and do its own learning regarding the process. If there are too many things they have to experience, and too much pressure to produce with no real resource support, then the result is very predictable—the process will fail. CIDM/QFD is too valuable to have this happen.

INTEGRATING ALL OF THE "VALUE DELIVERERS" IN THE COMPANY

The other issue along with internalizing a new process is that the company and its people usually are operating more in a "work group" environment—individuals from various departments meeting together to accomplish some work. They are not yet a team, but a work group—the various members are there to protect their turf or to defend their agenda—not a team that is focused on the same goal, each in a spirit of trust and respect. The need then is to align the necessary "value delivery viewpoints," each having a chance to level along the same experience lines and to then focus the "team's" efforts to better decision-making on what it really takes to accomplish a successful solution development. The need is to allow the team to contact the customer, as interviewer and as interview data reviewers, and as a multifunctional team discuss the customer data, analyze them for meaning, and then each reach the same level of knowledge while they develop the solution.

BECOMING AWARE OF NEEDED "CHANGES TO THE ORGANIZATION"

Usually, the team will need to focus on the rules for teaming, but more importantly they may need training on techniques to support them in doing their work. We often see the need to provide training regarding "teaming." LMA associates provide robust training on "getting results" in which they teach "organizational street smarts," "how to influence others," and "empowering yourself." This multi-faceted approach works to more completely prepare people to accomplish true teaming so that they are able to reach the level of high-energy adaptive teams (HEAT).

Other support training would focus on project management. The Integrated Project Management group in Belmont, California, support CIDM/QFD well with their Customer-Integrated Project Management training process. It's important to focus on how projects integrate across the spectrum including the customer.

Finally, an important skill that teams often have to acquire is that of problem identification and problem-solving. CIDM/QFD supports this at the macro level as part of the process, however, a foundation in how to do this at the micro level is also important.

Internalization Activities Checklists

Certainly, one of the biggest obstacles to change is the attempt to change without a plan. The implementation of QFD and the internalization of CIDM must also have a plan.

WHAT'S THE PROBLEM?

CSC Index, Inc., a Cambridge, Massachusetts, consulting firm, recently published in *Information Week* the following results regarding critical factors for success. We list these factors here because they subsume the issues facing companies for any change.

THE MOST DIFFICULT ASPECTS

1. Dealing with fear and anxiety throughout the organization.
2. Getting the systems and infrastructure in place.
3. Managing resistance by key managers.
4. Changing job functions, career paths, recruitment, or training.

We must be aware of these traps and get around them with ordered planning and patience.

From our experience some of the specific QFD and CIDM "limits to success" are the following:

1. The company does not believe that we have to do all of this front-end stuff.
2. The company thinks that all we have to do is provide the latest technology to satisfy the customer.

3. R&D and/or engineers and/or any unilateral group decides they "are the customers" and end-users in order to generate a list of customer wants and needs.

   Also, marketing will establish the competitive viewpoint on how the customer looks at the options in the marketplace.

4. The leadership team decides on a strategy of Ready/Fire/Aim—and feels they can react to the customer's needs after the product is released.

5. The team thinks they can react after the competition introduces their improvements.

6. The general feeling is: "The customer doesn't know what they want."

It is important to note that the culture will continue to perform as it has in the past even after they begin to believe the need exists for change. We should be able to reduce the impact of change by doing a superior job of planning and project management. Bill Kern and our associates at Integrated Project Systems in Belmont, California, facilitate and train for a customer-integrated project management approach. Their process uses customer understanding that CIDM provides in an integrated project management skills development that drives improved project results. As a foundation skill set it is important that a company have the most skilled internal practitioners involved in their initial projects.

Project Efficiency Enhancers

"TEAMTALK"

High on the list of responsibilities for project managers and facilitators is the need to report progress and to work in a project management structure. The need to keep track of information is paramount in providing periodic status reports, reporting the Ah-ha's that come out of the day-to-day interactions of the team (this step is vital, as many of the measures of success are found here).

The TeamTalk charts will be defined in more detail in part III, but we want to link the use of it here to the facilitator's responsibility for keeping track of the "value added" information from the CIDM/ QFD process and to the requirement for the project manager to use project management techniques.

TeamTalk meeting management techniques include keeping track—on flip-chart size paper—for all team members to see the following: (1) issues; (2) actions—who, what, and when; and (3) Ah-ha's. These flip charts then become a part of the meeting documentation and form the basis of reporting and project control.

MATRIX TIME REDUCERS

Another tool set that we have talked about and will be using to display our project information in part III is the software support tool for managing and archiving the matrices. We have used QFD/ Capture from ITI; it runs on either a DOS or Windows-based PC and the MacIntosh. We have it running also on laptops and take the software into QFD team meetings to support the data control during the meeting.

The ability to use this software has improved team decision-making significantly. It removes the "effort to make up the chart" and makes it a nonissue.

CHAPTER 6

Details and Expectations for CIDM/QFD Leaders

The characteristics that profile leaders of CIDM/QFD projects focus on those that determine the ability of the leaders to work within a teaming environment. The idea of teams has been a focus for about the last ten years, in one form or another, but it seems the value has not been realized by many companies. One reason may have been that since the focus of the teams remained internal, it concentrated on the politics of the company rather than on the realities of the market. Another result, then, of this internal focus is that companies perpetuated a "silo" mentality that fought for position against imaginary objectives, the groups of individual contributors were just "work groups," not true teams.

As we describe the characteristics that contribute to success, we will focus on a position of importance in internalizing CIDM/QFD—that of the internal facilitator. A description of this position is: (1) a person who has the respect of his or her peers and management; (2) that person need not understand our products or our technologies or even the manufacturing process, but he or she should understand the business we are in and what solutions we provide and the problems involved with providing those solutions; (3) each should be a people person—someone who has organizational patience.

Let's look, then, in detail at the profile of this facilitator, remembering that this profile also fits all of the "leaders" involved in the company.

A Profile of CIDM/QFD Leaders

MANAGEMENT ATTITUDES

This person should be strongly supported in this position.

There are times during the change process when he or she will be under attack from detractors of change. This person needs the confidence and support to keep the process moving.

The person needs the support of both the R&D and marketing management teams.

This is the hard one, as it's the one most often not present at launchtime. Unless the person can navigate around this, and/or the leadership team gives full support in the face of lack of support from R&D and marketing, it will be a real limiter to success.

They need to have responsibilities for other jobs reduced to allow for them to achieve the focus and concentration on the project and team that are required.

This is another hard one. Leadership will need to address this, and do some real juggling. But most often this person will have to do some "real time" informal prioritization of his or her workload, and the real good people get the job done.

Top management must understand the importance of the long-term nature of the CIDM/QFD internalization effort and therefore provide the "patience" required while it's in process.

One of the main jobs of the facilitator is to keep alive the commitment of the leadership and management team; to visit them often and to keep them informed; to interact with them often. They must assure the distribution of the meeting reports, include the Ah-ha's, the valuable learning that are indicators of success, as well as the limits to success—those issues that could cause problems in reaching project goals. Both are very important pieces of information that will serve to provide continued leadership commitment.

FACILITATOR ATTRIBUTES

The person should want to be or at least want to try to be the facilitator and should have enough information on what CIDM/ QFD is to feel that it is a valuable process.

Most often this person will have little information or very sparse understanding. The issue here is that he or she should be interested enough to try the first project. After the company has experienced some projects, then the person should come from the experienced pool of people who were in the project. Most often these people come from the engineering and/or the marketing ranks.

They do not have to be a project content expert.

The process is the issue here—it is more important that they be able to manage projects and work with management and individual contributors. If they are a content expert, they should not be an input to the decisions of the team and the facilitator both. They should learn from the experienced outside or inside facilitator and support the team in using the process.

They should like people and be able to provide "organizational patience" support.

Author Bill Barnard describes how he can distinguish the first-time QFD teams from all the other people that may be in a room together. He asks everyone to turn around and face away from him, and the "QFD teams are the people with all of the arrows in their backs." In the best-managed companies, the pressure during one of these projects is very strong. The person helping the team to make the process work cannot be one who is part of the problem.

They should have an understanding and a perspective for a process orientation.

The success comes from changing the process, which then changes the culture. The CIDM/QFD process works; it's this person's responsibility to get it absorbed into the company's culture. The job is understanding and being able to integrate the CIDM/QFD process into the other processes the company has and most often is implementing at the same time. The three main tools of the facilitator are process understanding, organizational patience, and people confidence.

FACILITATOR APTITUDES

Flexibility: The ability to make changes that do not impact results but make it easier to go with the flow.

The introduction of change is a perilous task, sometimes this leader will have to "imaginatively overcome certain short-coming"—in the resources available, in time constraints, in the impact of the change on personal lives. The job requires adaptation, compromise, and lots of being in the middle between the require-ments of the process, management, and peers.

Sensitivity: The ability to adapt and compromise. To adjust to people's moods, and energy levels.

The job is a rewarding one for those who like to help others learn. It requires understanding and perception—to be able to proactively know when pushing is the right thing or the wrong thing to do. Mostly, it's about being perceived as the mentor and often not getting recognized, and still moving forward to help others get the job done.

Self-confidence: Maintaining confidence no matter what.

The job will need people who don't require constant manage-ment direction, who can make decisions on their own. They know when the criticism is deserved and when it's not. They can exist for four to six months perceived as being wrong, only to be found as the project winds to a conclusion "as being right all along."

FACILITATOR SKILLS AND EXPERIENCE

In summary, the person selected for the facilitator responsibility, as well as any leaders, needs to have the following:

Team management and team experience.

Meeting management skills.

Training and/or consulting skills.

Process analysis skills and experience.

Our experience with this is that given the above profile and support for the person selected, a capable CIDM/QFD facilitator will result. You can't discount the person's having a desire to succeed either. Coupled with the above list of skills and experience, a strong desire to learn is also a worthwhile trait. Since CIDM/QFD is a discovery process in and of itself, learning is a key part of the process. It helps to be open to new ideas.

This person is *not* a superperson. Many of the people the authors have worked with in over 200 projects were just good individual contributors. During their mentoring, many marginal contributors blossomed and became very strong. The results are always that people grow and get better.

Middle Managers

"BIDIRECTIONAL" EMPOWERMENT

The word "empowerment" is one of the many overused words in the world of business today. The unfortunate circumstance surrounding its use is that it often implies that the supervisor should relinquish power to the individual contributor. So, often the words "Management won't empower us to do things" ring out from a team that is in the process of work. The issue isn't so much that management won't relinquish power as there is a need for communication links that provide a comfort in believing that the team will meet the goals management envisions, often that they even have a plan that will allow them to. The other side of the issue is that the team often believes that management "already has the answer" and they are just being patronized into believing they can "make a difference."

In the CIDM/QFD process, what evolves as empowerment is "bidirectional." The management team and the project team both focus on the customer, after spending time to properly answer the segment questions, and begin to answer the differentiation questions. They also focus more on planning the project regarding what the goals of the effort are. The result is that an orderly and structured convergence of understanding among the project members, the resource providers (management), and the customer occurs, and there is less suspicion and lack of trust. The effort becomes one driven by "knowledge and understanding" rather than emotion. The focus then is on the team "empowering" itself and then having information to communicate that meets the language of the sponsoring managers. The sponsoring managers feel less need to "look over the shoulder" of the team and more value occurs with less effort—all focused on the customer.

Teaming Checklist

A major issue confronting companies as they try to develop teams seems to be the level of expectations on what it takes to develop a team environment. It's important to define the possible "teamed" results that companies can expect. CIDM/QFD works to integrate individual contributors in "true teams" and eventually "high-performance" teams, which we refer to as "high-energy adaptive" teams.

The CIDM process defines teams at two levels:

Management teams—Developing the management products to set action strategy and priorities for the company action teams.

Company action teams—Developing action solutions for the company based on the action strategies and priorities supplied by management teams and customers that finally are supplied to customer markets.

Let's focus on the company action teams. (If you are interested in how management teams can use CIDM, *The Innovation Edge*, by Barnard and Wallace, is helpful with regard to CIDM as a management process.)

Groups of individual contributors trying to form teams typically go through stages:

First they are—
  Work groups.
Then they may become "true"—
  Teams as they focus on customers.
If companies develop the environment, they may become—
  High-performance teams—CIDM-focused—High-Energy Adaptive Teams (HEAT).

This part of the book will focus on the problems involved in moving beyond work groups. Work groups are defined as loosely coupled individual department representatives who just attend meetings and little else unless the team decision-making fits their goals.

The issues that confront a group trying to integrate and become a "true team" are the following:

1. They do not seem to be able to define what the team balance and/or composition should be. Often, the team is just a group of like viewpoints working to prove whose viewpoint is the most correct.

2. They do not seem to understand how to work with other teams or are unable to make a decision on their own. There are no "road maps" of how teams relate to each other with provisions made for horizontal, vertical, and cross-functional integration. They are often unable to make decisions without talking to sponsors outside of meetings—this comes from knowledge level or just being a messenger for a political "boss."

3. There is a low level of trust. Simply said, they are too busy negotiating their jobs to be working on problems.

4. The big "change issue" is that the move from "internal politicking"—even though they work for the same company—to

"cooperation" is a major effort. There must be an attitude change across the leadership. But how will this happen?

In order to successfully introduce teaming, the following checklist will help leaders evaluate how well they are prepared before they launch teams.

In order to prepare for the introduction of customer-integrated processes, it is important to review the company's strength and weaknesses in teaming. Figure 6.1 on page 105 will provide a worksheet to evaluate the company' readiness. Before you answer the questions, a little review of the questions asked will help.

In the question about structure in the problem-solving processes, you should review whether or not your people have had problem-solving training, or any other problem-identification education. The key here is replicatability and currency. If the teams were trained but never had time to apply the training, it is important to consider this when answering the degree of truth to this question.

To the issues of measurement success, you should consider the widespread versus selectively applied use of measurements. Also important is the credibility of measurements. Do you regularly set obscure targets and goals that are not able to be explained and then drive people to "make them happen or be replaced"?

To the issue of prioritization, is everything important (and therefore "nothing is important") or do you have a process of agreement on day-to-day project prioritization? Do the individual contributors understand the scheme of priority decision-making? Do you re-prioritize based on new data or plow ahead regardless of new facts to "complete projects"?

To the issue of understanding training competencies, do you have a "competency-based" training evaluation process, or do you do general mass training? How often do the team members have an occasion to use the training they receive? How much do they receive: two weeks a year, or two weeks ever?

To the issue of competencies through use, do the processes you provide training in become a way of company life, used at all levels, or just random division fads?

How about meeting management: Is there any, or do groups of people just get together occasionally and argue? Does the company work on a set of replicatable rules of order?

Has the culture over the years nurtured a military style of conflict and politics? Do the leaders promote the Fredrick Winslow Taylor School of "Separation" or the more contemporary "employee as a valuable contributor"? The answer here counts for more than the others, as this often is the stumbling block in internalizing processes that require adaptation, flexibility, and change. The answer can be improved if the leadership realizes this problem and has a firm commitment to change the culture—culture can be changed, culture is just the learned rules of the company. CIDM/QFD is a powerful culture changer.

If the answer to the above question is true, the answer to the question regarding "deep-rooted" issues between management is also normally true. Change starts best with the leadership showing good teaming.

Again, the answers to the above two question areas just covered both being true will lead most often to the questions about trust and confidence also being true—remember, no trust or confidence is the wrong answer.

The last area in question relates to the issue of accomplishing results in the introduction of teaming and any other change— if there is no credibility in managers following up on commitments, the net result is no results in changing the company culture.

So, with this introduction, you can evaluate your readiness to enter into teamed customer-integrated processes—there is no right answer. Obviously it would be great if you answered all the questions "not true," but the probability of that is not high. The answers should prompt you, however, to move into actions to achieve a better environment for teaming.

Figure 6.1

Leader's Checklist

	True . . . . . Not True
Little or no structure in your problem-solving process	— — — — —
Little or no measurement of success	— — — — —
Little or no prioritization of projects or problems	— — — — —
Lack of acceptance of customer contact by individuals	— — — — —
Lack of an understanding of how training in tools affects team members' competencies	— — — — —
Lack of competencies in tool usage	— — — — —
Lack of meeting management effectiveness	— — — — —
Deep-rooted antagonism encouraged by company culture	— — — — —
Deep-rooted issues between management	— — — — —
Lack of trust and confidence in management support	— — — — —
Lack of credibility of management follow-up support	— — — — —

A Sponsor's Checklist

What do I know about team issues?

Is it a realistic representation of cross-functionality?

Does it understand, and has it reached agreement on, its purpose and objectives?

Have I chosen a team leader who really wants the project to succeed using the CIDM/QFD approach?

Have I provided for just-in-time training and facilitation?

What do I know about the project?

Am I really familiar with the project objectives, the solution issues, and technology potentials?

Am I aware of the potential process implications that might have to be addressed?

Will I really support the potential for "problem prevention" that this approach will provide?

Am I really going to "change directions" if the indicators are that I need to?

Will I listen to the team or "tell them the old-style way"?

What do I know about the infrastructural issues concerning the rest of the company?

Who else in the company is using this process—are the team members stretched out with too many projects, QFD or otherwise?

Are we restricting CIDM/QFD efforts to the important and significant programs or trying to QFD everything?

Has the team defined all of the critical elements of the project—mission, scope, objective, market segment, customers, research required, the correct team? Am I aware of, have I agreed with, the answers, and finally provided the required resources?

Is there an imbalance in the team makeup, too many managers, or is the team unilateral in its composition?

A Facilitator's Checklist

From the preceding discussion, the importance of the facilitator should be obvious. The need for an ongoing person to be responsible to the company for the successful implementation of the CIDM process then requires that a plan exist for this. The definition of the responsibilities for this person is the objective of this section of the book.

We have described a position of internal facilitator that is part of the team and responsible for assuring that it accomplishes its objectives, using the tools and process that define CIDM. We define a requirement for an external facilitator to support this internal facilitator in the initial projects. What does this person need to know, account, and plan for.

The responsibilities of a facilitator cover different levels—from the preparation stage to the facilitation stage to the follow-up activity stage. For purposes of this book, we will define macro-, mid-, and microlevel activities that must be accomplished—"macro" referring to the entity level or division level, "mid" referring to the department or project manager level, and microlevel referring to the action and facility level.

PREPARATION STAGE

Macrolevel

1. Give presentation to functional management about CIDM/QFD.

2. Explain to functional management what their role is when the CIDM/QFD approach is used.

3. Support the development of choosing a pilot project and/or scoping any project using the process.

4. Support the team by interfacing with management and maintaining their commitment for the project and the use of these new tools.

Midlevel

1. Review with the project manager the objectives and deliverables planned for in the project. Road map with the project manager the information that will be evaluated by using the matrices and the measure of project completion.

2. Take a "first pass" definition at the "rules of engagement" that the team will work under—penalties, meeting rules of process, planned meeting time and frequency, etc. These will be shared with the team at one of the first two meetings.

3. Uncover with the project manager any potential schedule constraints.

4. Establish a training plan for CIDM and QFD as well as any foundation training the team may find important—like project management, QFD software, etc.

5. With the project manager and a marketing representative make a list of the potential sources of "research" that may exist in the company.

6. Plan the first CIDM/QFD meeting or the next depending on what point the facilitator has been defined in the team.

Microlevel

1. Talk about the role and definition of appointment of the "scribe" in the team. How the data are entered into charts, cataloged, and how team meeting reports are generated is no small matter.

2. Try and find a space that the team can lock and call their own for the duration of the project and even for future projects.

FACILITATION STAGE

Microlevel

1. Meet with the project manager after each meeting and define the meeting report topics and the responsibility for accomplishing this important activity.

   Prepare the agenda for the next meeting.

2. Proactively define any needed "extended team" expertise found to be needed during the meeting and prepare to schedule this expert for the next meeting.

3. Develop and review a facilitator meeting checklist.

4. Review the meeting to be sensitive to the issues of team dynamics—forming, norming, and/or storming? Create an action strategy and responsibility for accomplishing the needed contact.

5. Be flexible during times of action and flexible enough to let the team members enjoy the project. But be aware of any deviation from CIDM/QFD process procedures.

6. During meeting provide a status report to the team on where they are in relation to the plan. Review next steps with them and flexibly replan if required. Then communicate these decisions to the sponsoring managers.

7. Proactively contact team members and their managers outside of the meeting to do a check on their attitude and uncover any issues they may have.

   Make sure you point out successes and achievements in these contact meetings and in the regular team meetings.

8. Keep a journal of your facilitation experience. This will support continuous improvement and in process problem-solving.

FOLLOW-UP

Mid- and Microlevels

Do a postmortem on the project:

1. Review the learnings regarding:
   The use of the process.
   Team dynamics and communications.
   The results and impacts on them from use of the process.
   Customer impacts—long- and short-term.

2. Write a report or a "postmortem" and provide it to departments like: corporate quality, other facilitators, other projects.

3. Assume the responsibility for this effort yourself.

High-Level Success Checklist

TIPS FOR SUCCESSFUL INTERNALIZATION

Success comes from an ordered and structured approach to the internalization of the processes. The following checklist should help you in setting your priorities.

Necessary to Do

Provide the time—review the project importance load.

Give the team the controls—bidirectional empowerment.

Help define a scope for project.

Begin to change success measurements—make part of a team performance appraisal.

Provide the resource and time for obtaining "wants and needs."

Provide a team leader with an understanding and desire to use QFD.

Provide a QFD facilitator.

Provide the resource to acquire an outside practitioner to support the leader and the facilitator.

Understand the semantics of the team/company/industry—require a glossary of terms being used by the team.

Understand and work to internalize and integrate the CIDM/QFD process into a more robust "solution realization process."

As a leader, be the one that "wants CIDM to work" more than anyone in the company—and display this feeling publicly. Provide the resource to purchase QFD support software.

Should Do

Provide the resource to allow off-site meetings during the initial phases of the first projects.

Support and provide for truly multifunctional and/or multicultural teams. And publicly support and encourage "consensus" among those team members.

Require that the team provide you with periodic updates—if you don't receive them, find out why.

Understand the "imperfect work" pledge, and publicly support that understanding by frequently letting the team know they are in a "learning mode."

Provide the team with surprise "perks"—pizza parties, afternoon outings, etc. Show them you are rewarding them for their efforts.

Nice to Do

Provide an isolated CIDM war room for the team.

Provide foundation training to support the team.

It Is Implied It Will Be Done

That we are trying to establish a "mind-set" change, not just introduce a new set of "tools"—the flavor-of-the-year process.

Discover the answer—don't approach the project to prove we already know the answer. The objective is to understand the customer first, then make decisions on technology, cost, and other functional quality aspects.

Do Not Do

Introduce CIDM or even QFD alone to "settle" issues between departments, or influence a customer to "choose the company" for a sale.

Do not expect statistical answers—use the data to influence and guide decision as part of an overall process, not as a stand-alone process.

Don't measure the results in months—rather as a journey, not a destination.

Don't threaten the use of QFD to control adversarial departments.

Don't advertise an overemphasis on potential results. Overestimate costs and underestimate results.

Part III

The Project-Level Practitioner

Introduction

A practitioner is one who practices the methods. Practitioners are the ones who recognize the unknowns that are inevitable in implementing the principles and tools of CIDM/QFD. Without the benefit of previous experience to guide the practitioner, the opportunities for bottlenecks and failure are much greater.

Part III provides a comprehensive approach for practitioners to follow in implementing the CIDM/QFD model. It builds on the framework established in previous sections, which emphasized the top management commitment to change (in part I) and the midlevel leadership roles and understandings required for success (in part II). What follows in part III is a more detailed description of what happens when the practitioners are using the CIDM/QFD processes and tools. The description is not meant to be a dogmatic, rigid road map, but it includes the key steps that have been successful in over one hundred projects in which the authors have participated.

QFD, especially with the expanded view afforded by a CIDM perspective, will challenge many organizations to adopt a new way of thinking. This section embodies that new way of thinking and details what it means for the project team. It will demonstrate how the tools work and how CIDM/QFD has emerged to become an instrument for a deeper level of organizational learning, and how project teams may take advantage of this discipline. CIDM/QFD is all about making good decisions based upon customer values, and making those decisions fast and early in the solution realization process. Part III is essential reading for project managers, team leaders, facilitators, and first-time practitioners of the CIDM/QFD approach because it focuses on the tools and activities of implementation. In that regard, the elements of true teaming and project management are described in more detail in part III. Practicing the CIDM principles and sharing those experiences with others are how true learning takes place.

CHAPTER 7

Defining the Project

Project definition is the process of pulling together all the information needed to get a project team off to a good start. Part of this effort requires raising team awareness of top management's commitments to the change process in order to build incentives for accomplishing the project. The project definition phase is also when the team members align their thinking about their goals. It is the critical beginning of the process that creates true teaming, or what we call HEAT, high-energy adaptive teams.

Much of the project definition activity described here need not be restricted to CIDM/QFD projects; it can be used in any team-oriented project in the organization. In the case of CIDM/QFD, however, the areas in which the project will require or likely induce organizational or team changes are explicitly defined and agreed to during the project definition process. The degree to which top management is committed to supporting changes in the enterprise associated with CIDM, and the extent to which middle managers understand their new roles and responsibilities, therefore, are very important for a good project definition.

The manager or management group sponsoring the project (that is, authorizing the project to go forward) should form an initial "vision" of the objectives of the project. Sometimes, the vision is known as the "team charge"—what the team is charged to do. If management has been doing a good leadership job, as discussed in part I, and has considered the issues discussed in part II, this charge should be clear and agreed to by all people involved.

Recruiting the team may or may not be an issue, depending on your organization. But a good QFD team is made up of "cross-functional" representation; i.e., the team should have representatives from all the functional specialties that are needed to create and deliver the attributes of the value delivery proposition that the customer demands.

Before proceeding with the project, the team needs to come to an agreement on the customer benefit envisioned, the market segment, the project mission, scope, and objectives, and an initial idea of the effort to meet those expectations. This process establishes the aim of the BIG P, the broadly defined product solution system. Without this aim, there can be no efficient internalized learning. This early project definition makes the customer-oriented discovery process more meaningful. Key elements of the project definition activity include the product vision definition, the value delivery proposition, the mission statement, the scope, and the objectives.

The *product vision definition* heightens team sensitivity to the benefits required from the various customer viewpoints.

The *value delivery proposition (VDP)* distinguishes the key value elements of the product. It must be kept in mind at this early stage that the product definition is very fuzzy. The VDP should be as broad as possible and be clarified through subsequent qualitative customer research.

The *mission statement* focuses the project purpose.

The *scope* defines the boundaries of the project.

The *objectives* target specific outcomes of the project.

Product Vision Definition

In part II, we described and differentiated between a BIG P and a little p product definition. In this sense, the little p is that narrow thing that is purchased, used, consumed, or experienced by the customer. The BIG P product includes the *Little p* and can include an object, a service, a sound, a sight, a smell, a feeling, or a combination of these that more fully defines the value that customers in the value chain experience. The BIG P is a more complete definition of the total customer perception of the product. At this stage of the project, the definition only needs to be in terms of the customer's perception that is envisioned, whether or not the BIG P or *Little p* will be evolutionary (an extension or improvement to an existing product) or revolutionary (a strong departure from existing products or perhaps a completely new and different venture). The product's benefits/solution characteristics may be understood implicitly, but it's a good idea to explicitly describe these things in the vision definition, as well as in the mission, scope, and objectives. These benefits/solution characteristics have tremendous implications for the nature of the customer research to follow.

Throughout this section, an example (written in italicized text) will be used to demonstrate some of the elements of the tools used in the CIDM/QFD process. The example and its salient points explained in the context are fictitious, but will point out some of the subtleties that arise in using these tools in real applications. In this example, we have erred on the side of simplicity to maintain clarity and to highlight teaching points based upon our collective experience.

The example is based upon a team, the DB&N team, whose task it is to develop a new writing instrument. As you follow the example through, many of the real world scenarios commonly encountered will be addressed.

The DB&N team's initial product vision is shown in figure 7.1.

Figure 7.1

Product Vision Example for DB&N

The new writing instrument will provide the following benefits:

Be easy to manipulate and use.

Add to the prestige of the user.

Create lasting images.

Be available for purchase anywhere.

Be revolutionary in its concept.

Notice that the vision, though very general, does, in fact, set some goals in place. That the product will be revolutionary implies a departure from the norm. The remainder of the vision describes the benefits to be achieved by the product. These are customer-focused vision statements that ideally come from the management product. (See Glossary.) It sets the lofty direction and provides a point of departure for the team. It is based on the team's best available knowledge and is the basis for developing a more detailed view of the total value to be delivered to the customer.

Value Delivery Proposition

The value delivery proposition defines the broadest extent of the value provided to customers by the product.

It is important for the team to get a broad view of the product so that they are open to listening to anything that the customer may perceive as value. The generic picture depicted in figure 7.2 should

Figure 7.2

The Value Delivery Proposition, the BIG P

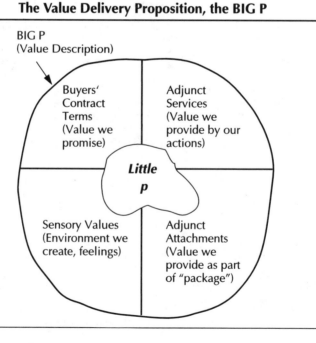

BIG P
(Value Description)

Buyers'
Contract
Terms
(Value we
promise)

Adjunct
Services
(Value we
provide by our
actions)

Little

p

Sensory Values
(Environment we
create, feelings)

Adjunct
Attachments
(Value we
provide as part
of "package")

be displayed and discussed to help broaden the team's horizons beyond the traditional view of the *Little p*.

The voice of value table described in more detail in chapter 9 is designed to elicit more detail from customers on the definition of the product value benefits important to them. We don't really know what the value attributes should be until we discover the scope of the customers' concerns.

Mission

The team mission is the step that gets the team focused on what they are about to do. The goal of the team at this stage is to clearly state and agree on the desired project outcomes. A project mission statement describes the project and its overall purpose and forms the boundaries for management support.

Four questions need to be answered in completing a mission statement:

1. What is the name of the project?
2. What is the primary activity of the project?
3. What is the primary product of the project?
4. What is the rationale for this project?

Figure 7.3

Mission Statement, DB&N Team	
1. *Name*	The mission of the DB&N Corporate New Products Team
2. *Activity*	is to design, develop, and implement
3. *Product*	a new and improved executive writing instrument
4. *Rationale*	which will allow us to penetrate the high-end market.

Mission statements are best when they are short, concise, and clear. Such concise statements are easiest to reach agreement on in a team environment. Try to avoid voluminous, grandiose, flowery statements. The details of the project will be expressed later in scope and objectives.

The key is to gain an identity as a team, be clear on what you are to do, what you are attempting to solve for the customer, and why. A clear aim is the goal here.

Scope

Closely related to the team mission, and sometimes included in the mission statement, is a statement of project scope. Scope addresses such issues as defining who authorizes the project and who is involved. Time frame, costs, and budgets are addressed, as well as the desired effects of the project. Target customers are initially identified here, together with the nature of the solution, that is, whether it will be an evolutionary product or a revolutionary product. Potentially, also, it could be a one-time special request.

Options to be considered ideally should be in relation to the feasibility of the technologies upon which each would depend. Pros and cons of each option are debated by the team, and solution complexity is discussed in order to get a feel for the technical scope that may uncover areas to be clarified with customers.

While a project mission specifies the overall purpose of a team, project scope defines its range of operations. Boundaries are set based on the type of product under consideration.

Figure 7.4

Scope of the DB&N Team Project

The new product will encompass the executive writing instrument category for the U.S. and Canadian markets and will help penetrate the (high-end) users market. It will be developed using rapid-prototyping techniques, leveraging what we have learned from launching products in Europe. The development budget is in the six-figure range and the product should support a family of products spanning three to five years in useful life. Although the product is new, its technology is not anticipated to be revolutionary. We will rely on existing, proven core technology and methods.

Straight and to the point, notice how the scope described in figure 7.4 creates a boundary. Again, there is no magic formula for exactly how a scope statement should be worded, but it should be based on reality and agreed to by team and sponsor. If any real constraints exist that are known, they should be identified here for inclusion as continued project barriers or for removal before moving forward.

Project Objectives

Project objectives describe in detail what must be accomplished to fulfill the mission within the scope of the project. They may include adjunct deliverables that are part of the BIG P concept or that provide leverage for other parts of the organization.

Figure 7.5

Objectives of the DB&N Team

In developing and delivering the new writing instrument, we will achieve the following objectives:

1. *Provide differentiation in the executive segment.*
2. *Focus on the U.S. and Canadian executive market.*
3. *Utilize current production capability.*

Use the checklist on page 122 to critique your project objectives to ensure that they align with your mission statement. Many times, the development of mission, scope, and objectives is an iterative process over time. It is critical, however, to reach consensus on these items before proceeding.

For example, the DB&N team did not initially reach consensus on the third objective. Ms. Smith argued that production capacity should not even be something discussed at this point in time because they could find some opportunities which may require building more capacity. Ms. Wright reminded her that it was indeed a corporate objective and should be kept in mind early and through-

out the entire process. Further discussion revealed, and the team agreed, that the current wording of objective number 3 did not preclude getting more production capacity if the market conditions warranted and it could be justified by the corporate management team.

Checklist for Project Objectives Using CIDM/QFD

- Is the objective linked to customer wants, needs, and expectations and thereby linked to the fundamental objective of customer delight?

- Is the objective challenging and worth the effort (seen as a stretch that it is difficult but not impossible)?

- Is the objective quantifiable and measurable?

- Are rewards and consequences for objective achievement or partial success stated or understood?

- Is each objective capable of being fragmented into subobjectives for incremental achievement?

After the team has reached consensus on the project objectives, document the information to complete the process. Care should be taken to assure that the objectives are not overly restrictive and that the team is still open enough for innovation beyond the traditional product boundary to occur.

Throughout our combined one-hundred-plus experiences with CIDM/QFD projects, the authors have learned the importance of being able to reflect frequently on the decisions being made and to adapt effectively based on the reflection. Revisiting, clarifying, and agreeing to new information as it is discovered is clearly a common discipline throughout QFD work. This is key in initiating team learning. No learning happens when preconceived notions of what we know are simply regurgitated in the project. The outcome focus must be new knowledge. As part of the overall

CIDM/QFD process, however, there is value in more thoroughly *refining* what is already known through the cross-functional process; also, "leveling" the team's understanding of project expectations creates greater commitment. Team members must commit themselves to being truthful and honest in their effort; this commitment to truth is the first objective of a high-energy adaptive team.

"Road Map" for QFD

Part II defined several approaches for QFD. Understanding various QFD models, selecting one for the project at hand, and visually communicating it to the team are the way to provide the direction and understanding required for a successful QFD project. Developing a road map also helps define the work breakdown structure for the project plan.

This road map is simply a flow chart using "icons" to show the high-level steps that will be completed during the project. The team will utilize the skills of the external experienced CIDM/QFD facilitator to develop this road map. See figure 7.6.

Training and facilitation are key here. Working together, the project leader and facilitator develop a detailed project plan based upon the current understanding of the QFD road map to be used, the mission statement, the scope, and the objectives.

Notice that the DB&N team plans on doing at least four planning matrices and returning to the customer base during deployment for clarification purposes. Because of a dialogue about the capacity issues raised earlier, the team has decided to include the deployment to production processes matrices as early as possible.

Figure 7.6

Road Map for the DB&N Team

1 Vision Mission Scope Objectives ↔ Understand Customer Needs

2 Reduce Data

3 Characteristics of the Product

4 Select Concept for Solution

5 Test with the Customer

6 Deploying Characteristics to Design Decisions

7 Making Decisions on Production Processess

Note: A key decision point in the project occurs after completion of the initial product planning matrix. Depending on the clarity of the discoveries made, additional matrices may be needed to further explore functional characteristics (see chapter 11).

Figure 7.7 depicts an initial project plan based upon the road map above. Each of this project plan's major steps is laid out in a project time line (represented by the dotted lines in figure 7.7).

The project plan can be as detailed as required—see appendix VIII for more detailed task estimates for project plans.

It has been our experience that the steps in figure 7.7 are fairly common in QFD work. They generally can be applied whether the project is a strategy, a physical product, or a service.

Figure 7.7

Generic Project Plan Based on a QFD Road Map

Vision, Mission, Scope, Objectives	/------/
Understand customer needs	/--------------------/
Reduce data	/-------/
Translate the VOC into product characteristics	/-----------/
Formulate and select best solution concept	/------/
Test with the customer	/-----/
Deploy characteristics to design decisions	/------/
Make decisions on production processes	/-----/
Continuously improve the solution and development processes	/--------------------------------/

Time ⟶

There are no hard and fast rules for "how long QFD takes." Appendix VIII contains project activity lists for the CIDM project with its applicable time lines. These are useful for starters. Learn the principles and determine for yourself the time that is most appropriate for you.

We often tell our teams that "QFD is forever," indicating that it is the beginning of a new way of doing business, rather than an activity to be accomplished in a given elapsed time frame.

CHAPTER 8

Leading the Team's Implementation

Building the Right Team

Building a good cross-functional team is a key step in project definition. Often during the mission, scope, and objectives process, the team discovers that some elements of expertise are lacking or missing. There is always a trade-off between having good cross-functional representation and maintaining a team size small enough for teamwork, decision-making, and consensus.

There are no magic rules for this. Depending on the nature of the organization and the complexity of the product, a core team is usually decided upon, with an extended team of experts who are called upon as needed. Normally working with the core team during first-time CIDM projects is the external facilitator. This key person should have CIDM/QFD experience and be a strong leader. The external facilitator takes a lead role in key meetings initially.

The DB&N team developed such a cross-functional team structure (see figure 8.1).

Notice that the DB&N project has organized into a core team and two extended teams. They felt that this provides the right amount of cross-functional representation on the core team to best run meetings, while clearly establishing other team affiliations that will be called upon from time to time.

It is also important to clearly establish the methods and lines of communication for the team. Will all communication happen in collocated meetings? Will e-mail be used? How often will the team meet? How will teams with international members be supported?

Team members can change over time. As the nature of decisions

Figure 8.1

DB&N Cross-Functional Team

Core Team

Team leader	Ms. Smith
Design	Mr. Weisman
Marketing	Mr. Marks
Manufacturing	Ms. Wright
Sales	Mr. Jansen
Internal Facilitator	Mr. Dent
External Facilitator	Mr. Barnard

Extended Team 1 (Technology)

R&D	Mr. Ernst
Plant 2	Mr. Block
Lab	Mr. Hale
Purchasing	Ms. Gray

Extended Team 2 (Sales)

Sales Manager	Mr. Jansen
Region 1	Mr. Carl
Region 2	Mr. Springer
Region 3	Ms. Dumas

to be made shifts with the increasing detail of a normal CIDM process, it is common to add needed expertise to the team. Additionally, as subsets of decisions need to be made during downstream deployment activity, it is usual to create new subteams for whole new decision structures.

Team Rules and Member Responsibilities

In addition to the functional specialties of each team member, "process duties" should be assigned to assure effective team meetings. QFD should become a key learning scenario for an organization.

As we have already discussed, basic duties are assigned to a team leader, a meeting note recorder and timekeeper, and the facilitator (QFD expert).

Team leader responsibilities are described further below. The team leader's primary responsibility is to assure that the team mission is achieved.

The recorder, sometimes called the "note-taker" or "minutes keeper," is responsible for documenting meeting dialogue. All of the information recorded on the flip charts, along with the subsequent QFD matrices, need to be archived. This important role should be shared by the facilitator and the project leader. Some teams rotate the in-meeting work among the team members.

The timekeeper keeps a watchful eye on the clock. Given the meeting agenda, the timekeeper announces time remaining. In this way, the team can stay focused on the subject at hand.

Important responsibilities for all team members include:

- Be on time for meetings.
- Be courteous.
- Listen.
- Share.
- Be honest.
- Keep your commitments.

These may seem simplistic, but they are important rules to live by.

A NOTE ABOUT DIALOGUE

Good team dialogue, and the ability to realize the leverage gained from this interaction, is important in assuring that the value promised by QFD is realized. Dr. Peter Senge, of MIT's Center for Organizational Learning, often speaks about David Bohm's work on dialogue,[1] and its importance in organizational learning. Why is this so?

It is important to recognize the difference between dialogue and discussion. Dialogue is about people putting themselves in a position to learn. It is about recognizing that language is practiced differently by different people and personalities. It is about recognizing that in order to learn from others, we must not judge, but temporarily give up defending our beliefs. Simply state them clearly so that others may respond to them, and then respond in kind to their beliefs. Through such a collaborative exchange, collective understanding and consensus may grow.

It's like applying double loop learning to conversation[2]—that is, reflecting on what is said and asking for deeper understanding of the speaker's position, rather than dismissing it offhand simply because it differs from our own beliefs.

When conversation addresses the differing positions at the table, seeking a more common understanding of the whole, progress toward group synergy of action is possible.

Dialogue is about understanding issues more deeply; it is about sharing others' knowledge and about allowing that knowledge to be voiced and understood by all. This will allow team members to be in a position to effectively express their ideas so that the listeners can understand them.

Dialogue becomes a powerful instrument in the hands of a good cross-functional team. Allowing time for dialogue to happen becomes a challenge in our hectic, pressure-filled world. It becomes the mechanism for pulling organizational memory to the surface so that it can be "mined." It becomes the method by which team recorders gain access to robust information for product planning. It's the only way to create an environment for true team learning to occur.

Recognizing the distinctions between dialogue and discussion is the first step. The second step is practicing dialogue principles in the context of QFD team meetings to achieve real breakthroughs in product development.

It is every team member's responsibility to learn and practice the rules of dialogue (see appendix II).

TEAM MEETINGS

When a QFD team is assembled, the new way of thinking should begin with a recognition of "team time." Team time is precious. It can be a time for tremendous learning, or a time of tremendous waste. It is not a time to take lightly. Preparation for team meetings, along with assuring value-added behavior during team meetings, is one of the most beneficial results a project leader can accomplish. A three-hour team meeting with six people is an expensive undertaking. The time must be used wisely.

QFD is a cross-functional discipline. Reaching a common understanding of requirements prevents misunderstanding and therefore costly errors and misdirection later.

Clear agendas should be prepared by the leader and the facilitator detailing everyone's role in the meeting. Team members should come prepared to fulfill their assigned roles and responsibilities in the agenda.

TeamTalk: The Information Binding Process

Strongly recommended is making notes, matrices, and process maps visible to all team members. TeamTalk (see figure 8.2) uses three charts for recording key information that emerges during the meeting process: issues/concerns, actions, and Ah-ha's.

The *issues and concerns* chart is a list of items that arise that cannot be resolved in the meeting. It provides a way to record vital concerns that need action for resolution.

The *actions* chart not only records the action needed but assigns a

Figure 8.2

TeamTalk Charts from a DB&N Team Meeting

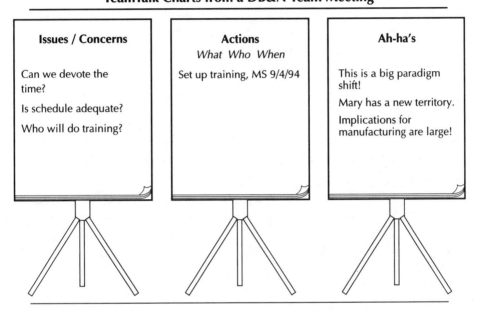

Issues / Concerns	Actions *What Who When*	Ah-ha's
Can we devote the time? Is schedule adequate? Who will do training?	Set up training, MS 9/4/94	This is a big paradigm shift! Mary has a new territory. Implications for manufacturing are large!

responsible team member and a target delivery date. These usually, but not always, follow from identification of issues and concerns.

Ah-ha's are discoveries made during the course of the meeting. Some discoveries are small, like "Oh, I never knew that!" Some can be breakthrough—"Wow, what an opportunity!" These provide a rich source of items for management reporting and help show progress during the course of project execution.

Notice that the DB&N team has documented an action to set up team training. MS will complete this action by 9/4/94. The action was driven by an issue of who will do the training. Also, the team wanted to document the fact that they all recognize the large shift in thinking this project will require. That information was captured on the Ah-ha list along with other appropriate things learned together as a team.

By keeping these charts active and current, the team has the opportunity to practice double loop learning. This is the way that organizational rules, policies, and assumptions are discovered, made visible, and questioned constructively in an interactive development environment. It allows for continuous improvement of the CIDM and development process.

As the CIDM/QFD project progresses, these charts provide a valuable record of the emerging solution concept as well as a valuable source of management report information.

The Key Knowledge Issues of a Project Leader

Project leadership more often than not makes or breaks the project. The fundamentals have already been discussed in parts I and II, and there is no question that an effective project leader is required for QFD success. If QFD is new, a first project effort, the importance of the project leader's role is even more prominent.

Although shared leadership is essential in a well-functioning team, it is still necessary to have one "official" leader: this is the project leader. Therefore, management and infrastructure support (administrative, computational, communications) must be provided to allow the project leader time to focus on the project.

A checklist for team leaders' responsibilities appeared in part II.

KNOWLEDGE OF QFD AND THE COMPANY

The leader should be familiar with QFD and with the company's product development process. It's *your* project team and *your* customers. Some knowledge of what is about to happen allows the leader to lead.

KNOWLEDGE OF THE TEAM

The leader should know the team members well. A frequent failure for QFD teams is the leader's lack of understanding, or knowledge, of the team members. This is generally so because it's the first time team members, who come from different functions within the organization, have worked together. Many times, organizational barriers are greatly reduced simply by the leader's getting to know the people on the team better and gaining their confidence. We call this period the "team join-up," and it can extend over a couple of months during early project activities.

KNOWLEDGE OF THE CONSENSUS PROCESS

The leader is responsible for the consensus process. It's important for the team to realize that differences among team members are normal and expected. Consensus is a state of commitment from all team members. It does not imply total agreement. The leader's role in gaining consensus is many times an art. It often requires moving information to the issues chart, and getting assurances of actions to resolve the issues off-line. The consensus process is a robust environment for discovery. For example, if a team has differences of opinion on an issue, the consensus process encourages identifying clearly what those differences are so that effective action can resolve them (see appendix II, "The Rules of Dialogue"). If the team is in the proper frame of mind, such differences should be viewed as opportunities to discover things never known, as opposed to opportunities to stand one's ground.

KNOWLEDGE OF COMMUNICATIONS ISSUES

The leader must keep the executives informed. It is not uncommon for the project leader or facilitator to take on the duty of completing the minutes. This makes it easier for assuring the creation of reports for management. The team must keep management aware of project progress, Ah-ha's (key discoveries made), and any limits to success.

This approach to reporting helps management realize how the QFD project is adding value in the organization, as well as providing technical insight. The meeting reports become increasingly more important as the customer research findings begin to be uncovered.

THE TEAM COMMUNICATION PLAN

QFD is a process that helps position a product strategically. For that reason, it is very important to all stakeholders in the development process, not just management. Examples of key stakeholders are purchasing, production, suppliers, distribution channels, and personnel departments. These folks are often not core team members, but may have responsibilities over processes that are affected by what is being discovered during the QFD project. A good question to ask is "Who will not have the opportunity to gain value if this is left unreported?"

Two-way communication channels are important so that the team can constantly evaluate its position. This steady stream of information back and forth allows for concurrent activities to progress toward the same goals according to the same criteria. "No surprises" are the watchwords for good reporting.

Figure 8.3

Communications Plan for DB&N Team Project

Meeting agendas will be published ahead of time.
The team will rotate the recording of the minutes.
Jim Smith will approve minutes.
Bob Marks will distribute the minutes via e-mail.
We will keep a project activity plan in the war room.
Information will be updated weekly.
Team meetings will be from 8 to 12 each Tuesday.
Remote team members will participate via conference calls.

Notice that the DB&N team communication plan is not long and elaborate. It is just a few clear statements verifying roles and responsibilities in the conduct of good communications. Note also the establishment of a war room. The war room is a powerful team tool to build good documentation disciplines, a lasting, continually evolving communication process, and a place for team esprit.

SETTING QFD PROJECT EXPECTATIONS

The previous steps in project definition help set the expectations for QFD. By the time the mission, objectives, scope, and road map are defined, a better understanding of what to expect emerges. Before beginning the customer research activity, however, it is important to have deliberate dialogue with the team and upper management concerning expectations. One of the first things that needs to be done is to address a team work issue concerning the "perfect work" reality. This team affliction happens when teams just can't move forward because concrete decisions can't be made early in the CIDM process.

Author Rick Norman has used a simple statement to help set an important work expectation, the imperfect work pledge,[3] because teams often get bogged down and even paralyzed when dealing with the inherently fuzzy information of early work. This is because it is difficult many times to be comfortable with the lack of definition or certainty before moving forward. Knowing that things will become clearer after visiting customers and processing the data only comes through experience and can be absent in initial projects.

The pledge goes like this:

"I do hereby acknowledge that, while learning, I and my colleagues will probably do some imperfect work. I further pledge to continuously improve my imperfect work."

The imperfect work pledge is a lighthearted way to internalize a continuous improvement paradigm with the team while keeping things fun. This is an important expectation to set because it allows for more open and free dialogue. Later meetings tend to get rather tedious, so a fun attitude helps break up the monotony.

The TeamTalk charts were designed specifically to manage this paralyzing environment and to document information for taking action. They also become a good vehicle for keeping expectations in line up and down the management chain.

CHAPTER 9

Identifying Segments, Customers, and Competition

Perhaps one of the most important steps in CIDM/QFD is selecting a group of customers from which to gather and understand needs. Everything else in the entire process depends directly on the quality of the decisions in this step. Following naturally from the project definition activities, mission, scope, and objectives, this step results in a detailed list of who will be contacted during in-context visits and other research methods. Once this group has been identified and their needs understood, we will also examine how competitive products and/or technologies compete for their choice behavior to buy our product.

The team's understanding of these data as they complete the project will determine whether they directly confront the competition or use other ways to compete with them. Knowing starts with understanding who is competing for our customers' "mind share." This is why we must not just listen to the voice of the customer; rather, we must put a process into place for understanding the choice-based decision-making processes of the customer.

Segment Identification

One of the most challenging, and increasingly critical, steps for a team to accomplish is that of market segmentation. The more competitive the marketplace, the more important it becomes to focus on a target market. This is a practice not normally performed by a cross-functional team; it has traditionally been the realm of the marketing departments. But a good team understanding of the process of segmentation can be very fruitful because all members share the same vision of the customers and understand the reasons for selecting the target market. This will be important when it comes to framing product concepts.

The segmentation step is especially important for QFD. If the group of customers targeted for interviews is too broad, it will take much longer to acquire the data, a wide array of needs will surface, and it will be difficult to design a product or service that satisfies all those needs. The more targeted the segment is, the more focused the needs discovered from the customers, and, therefore, the greater the potential to deliver a solution benefit that appeals to that segment.

An example of a successful segmentation effort at HP was the grouping of customers for the OmniBook, a laptop computer. The team decided, after understanding the potential markets, that a principal target market segment would be customers whose primary interest was word processing (document creation) while traveling. Note that the segment was grouped according to a set of similar needs.

It is not by any means an easy or straightforward process to segment markets. It is a process worthy of a good deal of rigor. This is one of the key steps in the CIDM approach.

"The relevant level for constructing a value chain is a firm's activities in a particular industry (business unit). An industry- or sector-wide value chain is too broad, because it may obscure important sources of competitive advantage."[1]

Examples of market segmentation criteria include:

- Geographical (in the southeast region).
- Task (all people doing word processing on the road).
- Perceived benefit of your product (how people group themselves according to how they perceive the benefits of your product, or express their needs).

The trick is to find a target market with similar needs in which to deliver a product or service profitably. This notion is known as "profit segmentation."

There are three main "customer wants and technology balance" questions that must be answered before we start a product realization process:

1. What are the "profit industry segments" we want to do business with?

2. What are the customer perceptions of our "positioning" in these segments?

3. What are the customer perceptions of the "benefits and value" they desire for these profit segments?

Effective segmentation is becoming increasingly important as a part of product planning. This is especially true with existing products in highly competitive markets. Effective segmentation:

- Provides a base for the matching of company and product differentiation to opportunities in the market for profit.
- Will allow for market entry and market investment decisions.
- Provides a more accurate basis for setting marketing objectives and strategies.
- Helps to identify "value delivery" needs to point the team in the direction of potential differentiation strategies.
- Can help to detect trends on more precise directions of the competition.

During the product release phase, having done effective segmentation will:

- Define the best presentation of product, price, promotion, and location.
- Allow for sales focus on the most profitable potential targets.
- Allow for more realistic results measurements.

Cascade segmentation is one method that helps us understand the potential for profit segment identification.

CASCADE SEGMENTATION: A VISUALIZATION PROCESS

Cascade segmentation is a free-form, yet structured, way to identify target segments. The criteria for segmenting vary widely from industry to industry and from product to product. An effective way to perform segmentation in QFD is to use a combination of structured brainstorming and an iterative visualization process (see figure 9.1 on page 140).

DB&N SEGMENTATION VISUALIZATION

Notice that the DB&N team has decided to combine the two subsegments, "offices" and "airplanes" (an estimated 80 percent of the heavy traveling managers subsegment). After some considerable dialogue, it was decided to focus there, since it may offer some opportunities for special promotion, and provide a big enough opportunity (80 percent × $9 million) to launch a new product.

This approach is similar to the "tree analyses" tools in that it will define a hierarchy of customer market subsegments. The process supports a team in visualizing the market and allows them to define their own taxonomy. The criteria for developing the visual image (cascade) emerge while thinking and talking through the process. Often, as more is learned through research, other, more accurate, taxonomies emerge.

The requirement is that along with the submarket questions, a numerical value and measurement of each subsegment potential are included. This will allow us to link the subsegment markets to define the best potential segments for research purposes. For example, in the DB&N case, the team decided to link the offices and airplanes subsegments for further research to see if there might be significant differences in usage there.

Figure 9.1

DB&N Segmentation "Visualization"

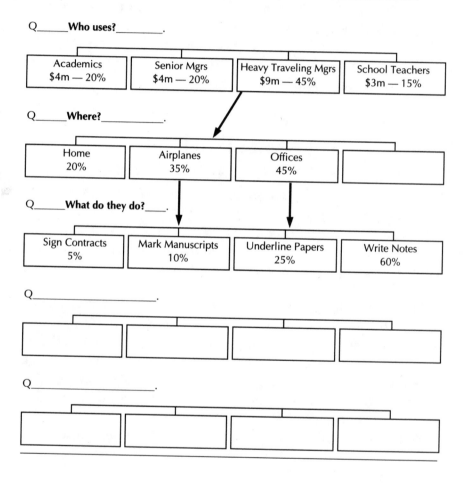

DEFINABLE MARKET

EXECUTIVE WRITING INSTRUMENT
$20m Opportunity for DB&N Team
(Total $100m with three competitors)

Q_____Who uses?_____.

| Academics $4m — 20% | Senior Mgrs $4m — 20% | Heavy Traveling Mgrs $9m — 45% | School Teachers $3m — 15% |

Q_____Where?_____.

| Home 20% | Airplanes 35% | Offices 45% | |

Q_____What do they do?____.

| Sign Contracts 5% | Mark Manuscripts 10% | Underline Papers 25% | Write Notes 60% |

Q_____.

Q_____.

The steps to completing this "visualization" approach are:

1. Brainstorm or use available secondary research to identify the definable market. Some influencing questions are:

- What is the overall need?
- What is the main customer problem?
- What is the key business process served?

2. The next step is to identify the subsegment cascade by defining the supplementary questions (the segmentation criteria). Some examples of these supplementary questions are:

- Who uses it or makes the purchase?
- Who influences the purchase?
- Where is it used?
- Why is it used?
- How is it used?

3. Next, we will define various segment priorities by linking subsegment questions. Guidelines for this process are:

- Do not use very narrow or broad definitions in defining your market.
- Don't define the cascade using products.
- Quantify terms as much as possible.
- Keep to seven or eight levels.
- If the team cannot reach consensus on the data, this could be an indication of the need for more detailed research, especially if they cannot quantify the subsegments. It could also be an indication that the segmentation criteria need to change.
- Be objective, avoid "same-old-way thinking."
- Do not attempt to make a decision at this point; that's next.
- Eliminate levels of questions that are not useful.

4. The final decision process involves quantifying and selecting a "target market":

- Examine the quantified cascade subsegments. Group subsegments that form potential target markets.

- The next step is to rank the various market segment "linked cascades" and to establish a priority while reviewing them as a team.

- The final step is to analyze the prioritized target markets and pick one by comparing initial data on the needs of the customer.

ESTABLISHING SEGMENTATION CRITERIA

The method found most useful in defining segmentation criteria is a guided brainstorming session. First, the team should, with the project mission guidelines in mind, name markets that they think would benefit from our solution. Second, document why those markets would be good targets. What emerges is a list of criteria that can be used to help identify target segments. Ask the segmentation questions (see part II pp. 56 to 60) to further refine the list. The objective of this effort is to identify the compelling reason the customer will buy our solution over all options they have.

Once the cascade is complete and target markets are identified, the next task is to determine who to talk to. One can then construct a customer matrix to help identify key customers to visit. This helps define our customer's "value chain," which evolves into the initial value proposition.

CATEGORIES OF YOUR CUSTOMERS

There will be several categories of customers for any product. Each category may have somewhat different wants and needs, which must be fulfilled by the product. Eight generic categories of customers whose wants and needs must be addressed by your product are:

Viewpoint	Definition
Planner	Determines consistency of the product with organizational policy.
Funder	Pays for the product, its installation, maintenance, and operation.
Auditor	Prevents misuse of the product.
Installer	Integrates the product into its environment.
Maintainer	Repairs the product.
Operator	Provides resources and supplies to the product.
User 1	Directly benefits from using the product but is not the final user (e.g., distributor).
User 2	Directly benefits from using the product.[2]

Using these categories, the team will construct their own customer matrix for their segment.

CUSTOMER DIMENSIONS MATRIX

The amount and type of information you require from each category of your customers depend on their involvement with your product. Three broad dimensions of customers exist. Since these dimensions are not mutually exclusive, a customer category might be divided into three dimensions.

- Customers that you *sell to* have to believe that your product has the ability to fulfill all requirements.
- Customers that you must understand who *influence* those who use the product, but their job may be affected by the product.
- Customers that you must *understand* who usually don't directly use the product.

Use this matrix to determine whether you must sell to, influence, or understand these customers for each of your chosen market segments.

	Segment 1	*Segment 2*	*Segment 3*
Planner			
Funder			
Auditor			
Installer			
Maintainer			
Operator			
User 1			
User 2			

The DB&N team used this process to better understand the nature of the information needed from each customer.

Figure 9.2

DB&N Customer Matrix	
	SEGMENT 1
	Executives Who Do Heavy Travel
Distribution Channel Buyer	Sell To
Shopkeeper	Understand
Executive on plane	Sell To
Executive in office	Influence

Notice that the DB&N customer categories have been adapted to their specific environment. Again the result of considerable dialogue, this step begins an ever-evolving process to gain a common understanding of the customers and their needs. Reaching this agreement on who the customer is specifically, and the nature of our need to probe, establishes a firm base for the next project steps.

Initial Customer Probes

Once the team understands the types of people in the value chain, they must start a process to formulate a set of questions. To help with this, the team uses existing knowledge to develop an initial set of questions to ask the customers.

THE VOICE OF VALUE TABLE

To help further focus the team's activity for the in-context customer visits, the team must get an idea of what the customer's choice importances are. A variety of methods can be used for this purpose, but a very cost-effective way is to use a voice of value table (VOVT) (see figure 9.3).

Figure 9.3

DB&N Voice of Value Table

I Want . . .	$100 Test	PENTEL	EAGLE	$1,000 Test DB&N	( )	( )
Name:						
Title:						
Company:						
Training						
Frequent writing seminars						
Needs no training to use						
Support						
Be able to buy anywhere						
Repair centers						
Immediate replacement						
Commercial Issues						
Easy to manipulate and use						
High image value						
Creates lasting image						
Adds to executive prestige						
Hassle free warranty returns						
Beautiful operation and feel						
Cost						
Reasonable price						
Unlimited warranty						
Quality						
Will last forever						
Feels solid						
Never fails						

The initial list of value delivery needs to include in the VOVT is developed based upon the team's best available information and experience. Care should be taken to assure that "our perceptions" of what the customer needs do not get in the way. Notice that the team used some "standard" needs area categories for this first cut at understanding the BIG P product wants and needs.

The VOVT is then mailed or faxed to fifteen to twenty-five customers to get an initial view of what they think is important. This is a critical step, for it is here that teams often find that their internal perceptions of what they thought the customers valued most are off a bit. This is a very useful phenomenon for teams to concentrate on for a while. It is important to establish a belief system that supports the fact that we do *not* know what customers want. An air of discovery needs to permeate that belief system. CIDM creates the environment for that discovery environment to flourish.

Focusing on Things That Matter

A key element of the VOVT is the $100 test and the $1,000 test (described on pages 148 to 149). This tool is valuable in understanding the customers' "choice-based perceptions" of the value and the importance of the activities that take place in the markets and the perceptions customers have regarding our ability, or anyone's ability, to meet their expectations.

This understanding is important in:

1. Gaining the team's agreement on what the "company value delivery proposition" is, the BIG P.

2. Establishing a focus and priority for developing the questions for use in the in-context visits' "interview guides" or other research we do—especially, what to probe for during the visit. We want to spend our time understanding the things that the customer uses as choice criteria.

3. Uncovering issues in our current value delivery system that if changed could affect immediate value to the customer and therefore the company.

CHOICE VS. SATISFACTION

We talked about the difference between "choice" and "satisfaction" in chapter 3 of part II. Figure 3.2 suggests the need to understand the attributes of our solution that will cause our customers to "buy." The team undertaking a solution development project needs to use all the tools available to be able to understand the "choice-based importance" that the segment uses. CIDM/QFD fills the holes that traditional QFD alone had with regards to this effort.

The best way to make sure we can predict the customer's "choice"-based importance is to utilize choice modeling approaches that have the following characteristics:

• The process must be able to utilize a sample size that will allow projections of conclusions to the whole sample. This number varies from project to project, but if we have made product requirement decisions in the past using only one or two key customers' wants and importance, the query of thirty to fifty selected-segment customers could be a 100 percent improvement in most projects.

• The effort to gain the data should be done anonymously. If the respondents know we are the ones undertaking the study, they may skew the answers. Maintaining anonymity is hard to do unless a company hired to do the work has the network to undertake the study globally—and enough people to do the work for all the clients they have.

• We should focus the study on the few variables for which we need to know importance. The ability of the team to have a good understanding of the differentiation potentials is important; that's why CIDM/QFD uses the "voice of value table" to provide an early understanding of where in the value chain the potentials are for providing customer delight.

• The study must be able to assure that all the respondents are provided with a survey document that assures they all have the identical task to perform. Again, the firm picked must have the best field data-gathering capabilities—this is the most important of all the decision-to-hire issues.

• The survey instrument must force the respondent to allocate a fixed number of votes to be used to answer the questions of importance. Often called the "constant sum" method, this approach forces the customer to weight the important attributes of the product, and also by doing this to reject another set or attribute.

• The study must also account for competitive alternatives in decision-making. In other words, some comparison of the attribute and the ability of our company and others to supply the attribute must be provided for in the study.

• The last issue is the ability of the supplying process to predict the purchase choice of each respondent separately, and then to be able to group the number of respondents and compare them with several different product ideas. This will give us a valid measure of which is the strongest.

No matter what approach we use, we try to understand and predict the percentage of customers in the segment who would make each particular choice given the available solutions on the market.

CIDM/QFD uses a scalable and flexible tool set for accomplishing this. The approach favored that is most accurate is one called "single unit market Models (SUMM)," as provided by Eric Marder Associates, Inc. To date, this approach has all of the attributes mentioned above and also can compare up to one hundred different attributes. Previously, the issue with using choice models in QFD studies had been their inability to compare the forty to sixty-five attributes most QFD studies work with.

Another approach for accomplishing "choice" understanding is the use of the $100 and $1,000 tests to identify customer choice preferences. Though not in the same class as SUMM's, this approach for a basic project team will provide an indication that will improve

QFD studies. When used with satisfaction study data, the comparison of choice versus satisfaction is often very eye-opening to the teams using this approach. An understanding of the customer's "choice"-based decision-making perceptions is accomplished by asking them to use dollars instead of satisfaction ratings to prioritize each of the value chain activities. Understanding their perception of the competition regarding each of the value delivery activities is accomplished when we ask them to reward suppliers of those value activities with dollars.

Thus, we ask them to tell us where they would spend this $100 to get what they want (what choice decision they will make) and then, using $1,000, we ask them to reward suppliers with this $1,000 for providing the benefits they want.

Using the VOVT in this manner begins the process of understanding the customer's mind when it comes to buying behavior. This same paradigm will be carried forward into more rigorous customer research later in the project.

CHAPTER 10

Key Market Research Tools

A wide array of market research tools is available today. It is important to distinguish between market research and customer research. QFD is about customer research; it is up close and personal. It is not about relying on "statistically valid" data from a "significant sample" using "preestablished preference" models. It is about going to where the customers "realize the value" from your product or service, observing them using it, and asking open-ended questions regarding their needs.

Going to the customer is a key strategy for world-class companies. Contrast this with arguments that "unskilled" engineers interviewing customers can create problems. Indeed, for the unprepared, it can. But the value to be gained from truly understanding and having experience in the customer's environment greatly outweighs the "lack of interviewing skills" sometimes experienced during first interview attempts by team members.

At Pierce and Stevens, a New York adhesives company, they created a "quality" ambassador program that allows any employee an opportunity to visit customers. Much is gained just from being there, observing the customers in their environments. Seeing, hearing, and feeling what the customer experiences will create a lasting impression. By visiting many customer sites, a picture starts to form in the team's mind of the unspoken needs of the segment being studied.

Preparing for In-Context Market Research

Using the data gained from the VOVT results, several actions must be accomplished to prepare adequately for the visits: Develop an interview guide, establish the interview teams, prepare to tape record the interview, set up the visits, and rehearse the visits and interviews.

INTERVIEW GUIDE DEVELOPMENT

The interview guide is meant to be just that, a guide. It is not a script to be read by the interviewer. Rather, it should be a rehearsal tool to make sure we ask questions in such a way and in such detail as to create a partnering dialogue with the customer. The guide should help create an environment in which the customer speaks freely about his order needs.

THE CUSTOMER VISIT

A visit has three general parts: an opening, the customer dialogue, and the closing. We call these key visit phases check-in, main body and probe, and check-out.

Check-in is the process of establishing a dialogue with the customer. At this point, we review the reason for the visit, the nature of the information we are after, and how we will use it with the QFD project. We try to "join up" and establish a comfort zone with the customer before continuing with the interview. The main body and probe section seeks a more-detailed understanding of their needs. General open-ended questions are asked first; more specific open-ended second. Probing is about asking the customer "Why?"

Check-out is the process of making sure the "door is open" for following up with the customer to:

1. Clarify responses.
2. Get importance understanding.
3. Just be a partner.

The comfort zone established assures future contact where we might follow up with more explicit requests for information.

The best guide format is to leave white space on the guide for observation notes. The notes are a key aspect of probing; we want to use techniques to keep the customers talking freely in ever-increasing detail to get better explanations about what they mean by their expressions. Effective probing comes with practice. The following example shows how an interview guide has been constructed in the format of the visit steps.

This format was used by the DB&N team to develop their interview guide.

Figure 10.1

Interview Guide for DB&N Team

Check-in: (opening the interview)

Hello, thank you for giving us your time today. As we mentioned on the phone, we are interested in better understanding your wants and needs concerning the writing instruments you use. We will use this information combined with the results of several other interviews to better create a solution for your writing needs. With that in mind, please say what is on your mind regarding your needs in this area. All that we discuss will be kept confidential. It will be used only by our development team.

Main Body and Probe

1. *What are the problems related to writing that you face in completing your daily work?*
2. *What are the issues you deal with today in using your current writing instruments?*

Probing and Backup Questions

3. *What problems do you face using writing instruments while traveling?*
4. *Are there any other needs you might have?*
5. *What comes to mind when you think about the experience of purchasing your next writing instrument?*

Check-out: (closing the visit)

1. *Are there any topics that we should have discussed that we didn't?*
2. *I will probably have to recontact you regarding some of the things we talked about today.*
     When would be the best time to call?
     Any times that we shouldn't call?
     What number is best to reach you on?
3. *We will also be contacting you to understand the importance of the needs we discover.*

Thank you very much for your time. We will be in touch.

Notice that all interview questions have been worded in an open-end fashion. This is important at this stage of research, because we want the customers to be able to say whatever is on their minds. Notice the questions avoid the words "pencil" or "pen" so as not to lock in to those solution concepts.

THE INTERVIEW TEAM

In-context visits should never be attempted by one person alone. It is best if they are done in teams of two. The interview team includes an interviewer who creates the dialogue with the customer and does the probing. The second person on the team is an observer who operates the tape recorder and takes notes on key points heard or observed.

This approach is recommended for the team because it provides two sets of eyes and ears. Two people can probe more effectively. More than two people on the interview team starts to look like a gang and it can be intimidating to the customer. An intimidated customer is not a customer who will speak freely about his or her needs.

RECORDING THE INTERVIEWS

Teams often wonder whether they should tape the interviews or take notes. In fact, both should be done. The goal of the visit is to begin to improve customer understanding. Tape-recording allows for eventual contextual understanding of customer wants and needs; note-taking assures the recording of observations that help get at unspoken needs.

To rely totally on manual note-taking will guarantee that much of the customer's actual words and phrases are lost to interpretation or incomplete notes. Taping interviews implies that the information on the tapes must be extracted. The most effective way to do that is to transcribe them word for word, highlight the needs, then move the needs statements to your data reduction process.

SETTING UP THE VISITS

During segmentation and while developing the customer matrix, the customers to be involved in the visits were identified. To set up a visit, the sales force can be a valuable asset for contacting the people and setting up the interviews. The "project objective" message to use with customers in setting up the visits should be developed by the team ahead of time so that the person calling will know how to position the customer for the interview and how to set their expectations.

The DB&N team developed a consistent letter to be used in soliciting interviewees.

Figure 10.2

DB&N Objective Letter

Dear ⟨name⟩:

As Senior Product Marketing Manager for the western region of DB&N, Inc., I am working with a team of professionals to better understand your writing needs. We provide creative solutions in writing instruments.

We are striving to be the best in our field. To compete effectively in the future, we must get close to our customers and understand their needs. We have a team working to better understand the needs you have in doing your work. Even in the realm of computer technology, we find that traditional writing instruments are still used widely, but we are convinced that significant improvements can be made when addressing your specific needs as a busy executive.

We would like to spend one day at (Company) and interview you and others individually for no more than 90 minutes each. The people we want to talk to fit the following profile:

- Business Manager: a person who must review, edit, and revise many documents through the course of his/her work.

- A person who travels heavily: someone who must complete that work, even while on the road.

We will share the results of our study with you once we complete our analysis. As an added incentive, you and your executives will receive a complimentary set of our existing multipen line of instruments, simply for giving us your time.

If it will be more convenient, we can meet you while you are traveling at any one of the following airports. We will arrange a hospitality suite to meet you:

San Francisco, San Jose, Cincinnati, Dallas, Atlanta, Washington-Dulles, or Chicago.

We will call you to schedule a time.

Thank you. I look forward to talking to you.

Regards,

DB&N Innovation Team

The team also developed a follow-up letter to be used to prepare the interviewee.

Follow-up letter to interviewee:

Figure 10.3

DB&N Objective Message Follow-up Letter

Dear ⟨Interviewee⟩:

We are pleased that you and your executives can spend some time with us at your facility on January 25, 1995. We will plan on meeting with each of you there in your offices on the time schedule you will provide us.

We'd like to understand your writing needs better. We're interested in things like how information gets written down to start with; what barriers you see today in using writing instruments; how you use your writing instruments today, and how you'd like your writing instruments to be so that you can do your job better. Specifically, we will be asking you about:

1. The nature of your work.

2. Processes essential to your work.

3. How often you use your writing instruments.

4. How you use your writing instruments.

5. The nature of the writing you do while traveling.

Please don't limit your thinking about current devices you use today. Think about an ideal world as well as the realities you're faced with today.

Thank you, and we'll see you on Wednesday at the time and place arranged by your secretary. Questions should be directed to Barry Jansen @ xxx-xxx-xxxx.

Sincerely

DB&N Innovation Team

Don't send the interview guide to the customer ahead of time. Try to make the interview as spontaneous as possible. It's okay to send a letter to the customer summarizing the information to be solicited. This will allow the customer to be thinking about the subject matter to be covered.

A plant or facility tour is important and recommended. It makes it possible to observe the environment in which your solution adds user value. If you're allowed to, take some pictures.

Allow some time between interviews. One of the things teams often try to do is schedule interviews back to back, thinking they can "get more data" that way. But this is not a time for haste. In that scenario, the interviews are rushed, the data begin to blend together, and the overall quality of the interview suffers. It's much better to leave at least thirty minutes between interview sessions to be able to reflect on the interview, write a summary sheet, and get set for the next interview.

REHEARSAL FOR CUSTOMER VISITS

Practice, practice, practice.

Edit the interview guide.

Practice, practice, practice.

Rehearsal is absolutely essential for new teams planning customer visits. It gives them time to hone their interview skills, work out the details of who is responsible for what, and what kind of signals will be used during the interview—for example, a note-taker may signal to the interviewer by leaning forward in a chair, indicating a desire to probe into an area.

Practice ways to probe effectively during rehearsal. Asking "Why?" is the watchword, but practice many ways to ask "Why?," namely, repeat what the customer says, ask, "Could you tell me a little more about that?," or simply say nothing and nod your head. All of these techniques "probe" the customer for more information.

The main job in interviewing is to facilitate the customer in expressing his or her needs. That's the reason for an open-ended approach.

Going to the Customer

The day has arrived for your visit and, if you have followed the recommendations up until now, you are well prepared:

1. You have set up a plant tour to see the areas where your product will be used.

2. You have asked specifically to spend time there just observing.

3. Your tour guide has agreed to be available to answer questions.

4. Your interview times are set and at least two of the interviews are with an end-user.

DURING THE TOUR

Not only should you focus on the actual process of the use of your solution application, you should also notice the environment. Is the location noisy? Dirty? Brightly lit? Warm? Cold? High traffic? What about the upstream and downstream activities? What communications are going on with the folks in the process? What interactions do the people have with others during the course of the process?

Be a sponge. Soak it all in.

ON THE HOT SEAT

The primary benefit of face-to-face interviews is that we have the opportunity to help the customer talk about his/her needs. Needs should be thought of as statements that express what *value* means to the customer. This is the heart of in-context visits: to get an understanding of where the customer places value!

During the interview, the team should do everything it can to put the customer at ease. Introduce the interview team and explain the roles. Review the nature of the interview, and develop a conversational atmosphere. Take as much time as it takes to get comfortable.

Begin the questioning. Probe, probe, probe! Try to keep the customer talking about each area for a length of time. The tendency for beginners is to move on to the next issue when conversation slows, rather than trying to really listen for opportunities to probe for understanding of needs. The reason for probing is to get the customer to express his or her needs and wants. Try to look for opportunities to get the customer to describe their sources of value:

1. Express benefits (of the solution).

2. Describe problems they are having and potential fixes.

3. Describe the peer pressures they feel in situations and how those pressures might be alleviated.

This line of questioning will give us better insight into customer *needs*.

The note-taker should also be prepared to bail out a conflict issue between the interviewer and the customer, as well as to participate in the closing summary. This gives ample opportunity for the observer to probe into areas at the end of the interview if no opportunities existed earlier.

Interview Closing Summary

Specifically mention that it may be necessary for us to contact them to follow up and get more detailed information on what we have discussed. Write down specifics of when and how to reach the customer. Nothing is more effective than a conversation with the customer in quiet time, just as he or she requested.

What to Do with All That Data

One of the big surprises teams realize is the huge volume of data that comes out of twenty or so interviews. It can be a bit daunting at first, but as the process of reducing and synthesizing the data begins to unfold, the team gains a great deal of insight and perspective.

Transcribe the tapes. Outside services are available for this, but some teams use their own internal administrative resources.

Once the transcriptions are available, the team should work together to highlight the needs statements and transcribe them to cards. This is the most common way to do the affinity process. Each of the cards should express a customer need or want, only one idea each, and be written legibly so that it can be viewed from about five feet away. On the card should be a "linking code" that will tag the card back to the interview. Codes can include name, title, company, date of interview, transcript page number, and paragraph number. The idea for the code is to be able to trace the customer statement in case clarification is needed later and to be able to sort information according to customer demographics.

THE VOICE OF THE CUSTOMER TABLE (VOCT)

Many times it is difficult for teams to understand the difference between a statement that describes a need and a statement that describes something else—a solution, a target value, or a product characteristic. All of this information is important to better understand the contextual framework surrounding customer needs, but at this juncture of the QFD project, we are trying to glean from the interview context just what the customer needs are.

A tool that enables this process is known as the "voice of the customer table (VOCT)" (see figure 10.4). As a minimum set of data to analyze, the VOCT should include columns for:

"Identification code," a card number assigned to identify the customer;

"Current wording," the actual words identified initially as needs;

"Definition," a column identifying what the statement is (a solution, measure, need, or other); and

"The real need," a column recording the team's conclusion concerning the real need.

The objective of the VOCT is to separate the needs statements from the many things customers say so that we can begin to focus only on the needs, yet preserve the contextual frame in which the need was expressed. When captured in a computer database, the VOCT provides a valuable structure for further analysis and understanding of the customer environment.

Notice that on line one of the table, the team extracted a direct quote from this customer, "Writes like a dream." It does describe a benefit, but what exactly does that mean? To understand it fully, the team must look within the context of gripping the instrument and the actual contact with the paper. All this information adds meaning *to the voice item describing the need.*

The VOCT is used by the team to analyze the customer voice data. It provides a rich learning environment for the team because they discuss the customer "verbatims" and record the context

Figure 10.4

DB&N Example VOCT

Card #	Current VOC Wording	What kind of comment is it?*	Ideas in context	The Real Need
32	"Writes like a dream"	benefit	smooth contact easy flow easy grip	"Writes like a dream" easy to hold while writing
33	"Needs 4 lead types"	solution + target value	multiple uses ease to switch	easy to switch for multiple uses
34	"good impression"	feeling	looks good, how friends feel when I loan it out "like I have $$$"	"create good, expensive impression when loaned"

* Solutions, Measures, Others?

within which the words expressed by the customer exist. Practical use of such tools provides a deeper understanding of the customer and the operating environment.

A good example of effective use of VOCTs comes from Raychem Corporation.[1] In that study, the team found many words and phrases from customers that were really design solutions. The VOCT helped them interpret those solutions statements to ascertain the underlying customer needs.

Marilyn Liner of Raychem Corporate Quality was the QFD facilitator on the project and has been instrumental in helping other Raychem teams implement QFD. Talking about VOCT's, Marilyn says:

"It's been our experience at Raychem that the VOCTs are an excellent way to help teams understand what the 'Voice of the Customer' is. The VOCT sorts the customer's words into recognizable parts so that team members can distinguish between needs and other things customers talk about. Using the VOCTs points out where the teams have been weak probing in the interviews and helps them become more proficient at probing."

Steps for using the VOCT:

1. Get the VOC on tape.
2. Transcribe tapes.
3. Capture words and phrases.
4. Record context columns.
5. Dialogue to agree on "wants" and "needs."
6. Finalize "wants" and "needs."

Once the need statements (which may number in the hundreds) have been extracted from the interviews, analyzed in a VOCT, and assembled into a list, the team must then further reduce the data to be able to manage the next QFD steps more effectively.

THE PROCESS OF DATA SYNTHESIS

One of the main activities of the QFD project is the process of reducing and synthesizing the many statements that customers make in their interviews into the wants and needs items to be used in the "House of Quality" QFD matrix. The most common tool for doing this is the affinity diagram. Also available are computerized technologies that reduce and synthesize data through "text analysis" processes. Affinity diagramming is fairly simple and straightforward and can be used effectively by the QFD team with fewer resources.

Affinity Diagramming

Prior to beginning the affinity process, assemble the cards representing the needs list from the VOCT. All the cards are put on a table randomly (if "sticky notes" are used, they can be put on a wall). Ideas that are related are then put together into natural groupings. This should be done in a team environment. These groupings represent a total segment view of the key need areas.

Rules for the affinity process:

1. Silently at first, move cards into natural groups.
2. Observe cards being moved constantly and explore why.
3. If a card moves between two locations frequently, duplicate it and leave a card in both places.
4. Once groups of cards have been formed, try to pick one card that best describes the whole group to serve as header card. If not possible, work with the team and create one that best captures the idea of the whole group.
5. Preserve the actual words of the customer as much as possible.
6. Repeat the process with the header cards (starting at step one) to form higher-level groups.
7. Record the final affinity in a tree diagram (see figure 10.5).
8. Keep the "tree" visible during subsequent meetings.

Once the tree is constructed from the affinity process, it becomes much easier to summarize and focus on key needs areas of the customers.

In the case of the DB&N team, note that after grouping all the needs statements from all customers in this segment, it is clear that the four main areas of need deal with "writes and handles like a dream, creates a good, expensive impression, easy to order and replace, and protect the environment." The detail of what all that means is clearly displayed by the tree. That detail will become important later on when establishing a company response to satisfy those needs. In this example, the team discovered *that many*

Figure 10.5

A Three-Level Tree Resulting from
an Affinity Process for DB&N Segment

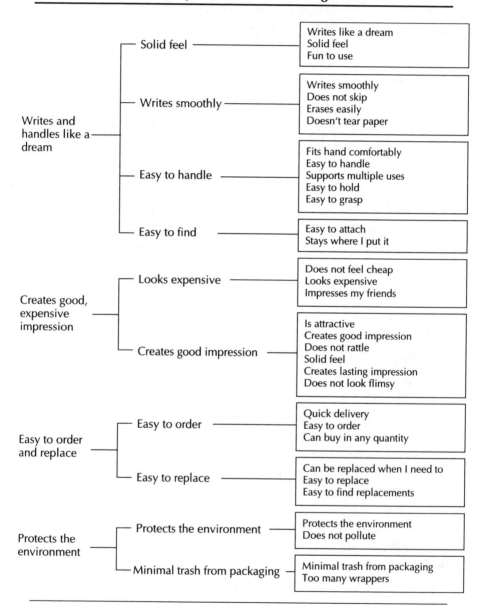

customers talked about protecting the environment, a newly estab-
lished focus.

One level of the affinity must be selected as the final needs list. The secondary level usually provides the best level of detail, but there is no magic rule of thumb for this. A good target number is twenty-five to fifty wants all at the same level.

The last step is to preserve the wants and needs in some form of database. The manual affinity process is a good way to get a cross-functional learning environment, but as teams mature with the process, more powerful tools can be used.

Text Analysis

More sophisticated software tools are available to help extract needs statements from the transcribed text of the customer interview qualitative data. One tool we recommend for this more advanced form of research is CustoWare™, developed and marketed by Polansky Incorporated.[2] CustoWare™ takes the "raw" text as it is and then uses content analysis, neurolinguistic and semantical analyses, and quantitative methods to "understand" customer information. The output is a database the team can use on its own computers, which provides customer information "at their fingertips." It will appreciably reduce the time spent in doing data reduction and affinity diagramming. Its expense is definitely worth the time reduction and accuracy improvement, and the time it saves can be applied toward doing a more complete CIDM/QFD project. The bottom line is it will allow the team to spend more time developing a more "delightful" product concept.

Focusing on What Really Matters

Once the final needs list has been established, the team must determine for all items on the list a relative degree of customer importance and competitive perception and incorporate that data into the process. In other words, we must ask the customer base to

"Consider this entire list and tell me what's most important. Also tell which companies are doing the best job in these areas."

The goal is to focus on what is most important to the customer, address those areas first, and expend resources delivering value to the customer in a prioritized fashion. The team must do that in the context of what the competition is doing, so that the customer *chooses* you over the competition.

Many methods exist today for gathering importance and competitive data. Unfortunately, most are based on a process of averaging satisfaction data of individual attributes rather than "choice" trade-offs across many, up to one hundred, attributes. The averaging process reduces the usefulness of the data.

A more robust approach is one that focuses on understanding choice behavior, described earlier, which is based on the concept that people use choice decision-making processes that are different from processes they use to describe satisfaction. We discussed this difference in part II. There is a whole range of methods to determine this customer choice behavior.

Least accurate, but relatively easy to do, are satisfaction surveys. These typically ask the customer to score each need, on a scale of 1 to 5, on its level of importance. The customer is also asked to rate each competitor from high to low on performance on each item. The results are then averaged across a customer population. This approach gives some insight into what customers feel are important and how we stack up against the competition, but the average values can be misleading if individual customer responses are not analyzed thoroughly.

A slightly more accurate—and fairly easy—method is similar to the one described above. Rather than asking the customer to place an importance/performance number next to each need item, we ask them to rank the list from high to low. Since the items are ranked relative to each other, it provides a bit more precise information about customer preference. This method is difficult, however, when the item list gets much over ten to twelve items.

More accurate still, but still fairly easy to administer by the project team, is a method aimed at getting a better understanding of customer preference *choice*. This method asks customers to distribute a fixed amount of money across the list of items based on where they would spend their money. As described in the VOVT section, the CIDM model uses a technique called the "$100/$1,000 test." Customers are first asked to distribute $100 to the items they prefer to have the most (customer importance "choice"). They are then asked to distribute $1,000 across the set of attributes to reward companies doing a good job in each area (competitive perception "choice"). They can distribute the money any way they want. The results are still averaged, but the choice range is wider and we force trade-offs between items; thus the results are a better indicator of how customers will make choices if all benefits listed were available for "purchase."

Figure 10.6

DB&N Example of $100/$1,000 Test Results

I Want . . .	$100 Test	PENTEL	EAGLE	$1,000 Test DB&N	(Seiko)	( )
Name:						
Title:						
Company:						
Writing Function						
Solid feel	5	100				
Easy to handle	10		50			
Easy to find	5		50			
Writes smoothly	10	100				
Impression						
Looks expensive	5	100	50			
Creates good impression	25	100			200	
Ordering/Procuring						
Easy to order	5			50		
Easy to replace	5			50		
Environment						
Protects the environment	10		50			
Minimal trash from packaging	20		100			

Notice the results of the DB&N example in figure 10.6 (on page 167). It is a good idea to send a description of each want along with the test form to assure understanding of what each means. The team will also have to decide whether to include their existing product as one of the choices in the $1,000 test. Note the "write in" blanks for allowing customers to list companies they want to reward for good performance. The final decision the team must make is how to summarize the results of the test. There are no magic formulas for this. A simple addition of all responses works very well.

The $100/$1,000 test is a simple and manageable means to better understand customers' choice behavior.

Most accurate, but more sophisticated and costly, is choice modeling. Choice models are built on a sophisticated database of customer choice comparisons, asking pairwise questions on all the attributes. Choice models give much more capability to play "what-if" analysis in a proactive manner.

CHAPTER 11

CIDM/QFD Essence: The Logical Chain of Decisions

At the very heart of the CIDM/QFD process is a rigorous, structured approach to decision-making. A matrix, discussed later in this chapter, is used to explore the relationships between key elements of quality. Cause-and-effect relationship exploration provides a format and environment to gain a deeper understanding of the issues involved in satisfying customers.

Deploying the "Voice of the Customer"

Figure 11.1 is a generic map of the CIDM/QFD process. As discussed in part II, several different models exist for developing the QFD matrices. The key, however, is not to copy any of the models verbatim. Rather, understand the principles involved and adapt them to your needs. The generic map is an attempt at describing the fundamentals involved with the deployment concept within a QFD framework. It shows the logical chain of decisions used throughout the CIDM/QFD process. Note that this "generic map" is formed in a circle, signifying the continuous nature of CIDM/QFD.

The matrices used throughout QFD help us understand what to do to address the needs of the customer with our solution. As you peruse each phase, keep in mind that each matrix is a discovery process just like the in-context visit process. The matrices are

Figure 11.1

The Generic Deployment Model, Integrated Customer Understanding

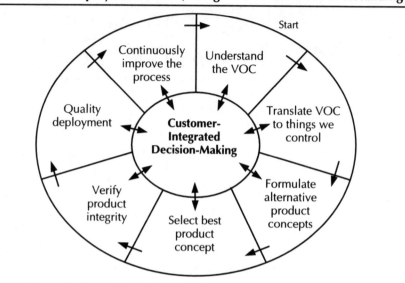

merely the vehicle by which a cross-functional team learns and understands together. There may be more or fewer matrices used than described here; it depends on the aim of the project, the degree of understanding needed, and the resources available during the project.

ANALYZING AND UNDERSTANDING THE "VOICE"

As the results of the in-context visits begin to be understood, the "voice of the customer" database will be refined. The details of the wants and needs from the VOCT described earlier provide robust "hints" as to the meaning of the customers' demanded quality.

TRANSLATING THE VOC INTO WHAT WE CAN CONTROL

Product Planning Matrix for Characteristics

There are a variety of matrices that can be constructed to translate the voice of the customer. There is no magic formula for any of these matrices. Their main purpose is to help us understand what we must do to satisfy the customer. They help us do this in two ways: by forcing us to look at relationships among things, and by helping us prioritize based upon those relationships. Customer "verbatims" are very useful in helping the team to formulate quality characteristics for the solution to be developed, as well as their target values. This information is useful throughout the processes of translation and deployment.

Let's explore a few decision matrices to get an idea of how they work. The most common matrix translates the VOC to quality characteristics (aka "measures"). Figure 11.2 shows an example of Product Planning.

This matrix is also known as the "House of Quality." Its primary purpose is to translate the customer wants and needs into things we can control to deliver the demanded quality. Here is where the team's "solution strategy" begins to form because the matrix provides the structure to enable decision-making.

In supporting this "decision-making environment," the matrix helps the team explore:

1. What's most important to the customer.
2. Customer perceptions of the competition.
3. What we must do to deliver value.
4. The impact of each quality characteristic on each need.
5. Potential bottlenecks in delivering value.
6. A prioritization of value quality characteristics.
7. An understanding of existing solutions.

Notice that on the right-hand side of the matrix in figure 11.2 are the data from the $100/$1,000 test. Across the top are the "company

Figure 11.2

DB&N Product Planning Matrix for Measures

Product Planning for Measures

CORRELATIONS Legend

Strong Positive	●	9
Positive	○	3
Negative	✕	-3
Strong Negative	✲	-9

WANTS vs. MEASURES Legend

Strong	●	9
Moderate	○	3
Weak	△	1

QUALITY CHARACTERISTICS	"Feel" panel results	"Shape & Fit" Panel Test	Number of attachment modes	Mark application pressure	Material quality index	"Impression" panel test	Time to place order	Time to replace	Amount of recylable material	Amount of packaging	Choice Importance	$1,000 Test	Pentel	Eagle	DB&N
Direction of Improvement	↓	•	↑	•	↑	↑	↓	↓	↑	↓					
CUSTOMER NEEDS															
Solid Feel	●	○		△		△					5	100			
Easy to handle		●	○	△		○				△	10		50		
Easy to find			●			△					5		50		
Writes smoothly		○		●							10	100			
Looks expensive			△		●	○					5	100	50		
Creates good impression	△	△	△			●		○			25	100			
Easy to order							●				5			50	
Easy to replace							△	●			5			50	
Protect the environment									●	●	10		50		
Minimal trash from packaging						△			○	●	20		100		
Choice Technical Importance	70.0	160.0	105.0	105.0	45.0	300.0	50.0	45.0	225.0	280.0					

Maximum Value = 300.0
— Choice Technical Importance
Minimum Value = 0.0

Target Value	.010 index rating	10 panel score	three +	like Parker Lux	10 panel score	10 panel score	5 min.	5 min.	100%	0 oz.

Competition Analysis

Pentel	.010	5	1	std. ball	hi	5	7	can't	30	10 oz.
Eagle	.020	2	1	std. ball	lo	5	10	can't	35	8 oz.
Seiko	.005	7	2	roller	very hi	7	n/a	12	10	12 oz.

Minimum Value = 25.0
Maximum Value = 150.0
○ △ ● — Pentel / Eagle / DB&N

response" quality characteristics. The relationship symbols in the center link our response to the customer needs.

For example, in the DB&N matrix, there is a strong relationship between the "easy to handle" customer want and the "Shape & Fit Panel Test" company response quality characteristic. This means that as the company strives to meet the target value of 10 on a panel test, there is a strong impact on meeting the need of "easy to handle."

The product planning matrix is the most common QFD matrix companies complete. It is a powerful planning tool in which information can be assimilated and discussed by a team.

Marilyn Liner of Raychem talks about the product planning matrix (PPM): "A key point about the PPM is not to take the results of the matrix arithmetic as an exact priority list. Rather, these numbers should serve as the basis for discussion. I strongly believe that the team understanding that results from completing the PPM (or any QFD chart, for that matter) is far more important than creating a perfect matrix."

Target Value Analysis Ladder

Perhaps the most important aspect of the product planning matrix as it relates to its "measures" is the process of establishing "target values" (see bottom of matrix) for those measures. Measures have a unit of measure, a direction of improvement that is controllable by the firm, and a target value that can be evaluated.

We find that a two-step process is best when establishing the target values because in practice many of the product measures' target values are not specifically known or are indeterminate from the information currently available. The preliminary target values can be set by considering several factors.

Externally derived—factors outside the company's control:

- A "reverse engineering" of the competition's abilities in delivering their "value delivery proposition."
- An understanding of the "best or optimum" irrespective of the supplying source—other industries, etc.
- Consideration of the potential opportunities for "differentiation."

Internally defined—factors within the company's control:

- Our current "values" as delivered in our solution.
- Complaints regarding these "as-delivered" solutions.
- Our own abilities to accomplish results—
    Technical competencies of our people.
    Process issues in achieving results.

The final values are set using external experiments to understand the customer using "choice" decision research.

The steps to define target values are:

1. Define the factors and attributes of the characteristics we need to consider.

Attempt to set preliminary target values for as many of the "characteristics as possible from the secondary data, market knowledge of the team, and in-context market research transcriptions and reductions. This is a first-pass evaluation on our company's ability to meet them. The first pass should be tracking using TeamTalk charts and preliminary target value "ladders" as shown in figure 11.3.

TeamTalk tracked.

Preliminary characteristic analysis "ladders."

2. Define where we will acquire the data.

We should gather data to be able to compare the following variables in the "target value" equation:

(1) Competitive data on the "characteristic"
    A. Identification of our competitors
    B. Collection of data
    Derived from:
        Product Marketing Documents
        Secondary research
        Primary research
        Reverse engineering
        Customer contact experience

(2) An understanding of our competencies
    A. An understanding of our "performance" in the marketplace
       Derived from:
           Sales reports
           In-context customer visits
           Warranty data
           Trade journals
           Reverse engineering
           Predictive models
    B. An internal assessment on the probability of accomplishing
       the characteristic
         An understanding of technology's ability to accomplish
       the characteristic
(3) Any survey data—primary and secondary
(4) Actual products and services experiences

3. The next decision is how to act on the data we decide to use.

If we are defining final target values, usually done after the completion of the product planning matrix, we will need to ask how our decisions regarding the "final target value" have affected the "priority decisions" we have calculated in the QFD matrix.

A tool to help organize these decisions to be made regarding target values is the target value ladder. The DB&N team developed the ladder in figure 11.3 on page 176.

Product Planning Matrix for Functions

Sometimes in completing the product planning matrix for measures, marketing and engineering team members don't always see eye to eye on the target values. Discussions using the "target value ladders" surface these differences of opinion. Another matrix will support this decision-making. This matrix, known as the "function matrix," relates the functions the solution must perform to the customer needs.

At this stage of decision-making, the function matrix helps the team interaction and discussion be more conceptual in nature and less solution-specific. By doing both types of product planning

Figure 11.3

DB&N Example Target Value Ladder

					Target Value
Symbols	Current Values	-	CV	=	10 minutes
	Competitors	-	A	=	10 minutes
		-	B	=	7 minutes
		-	C	=	__n/a____
		-	D	=	__n/a____
	Target to Differentiate	-	TTD	=	5 minutes
	Target to Plan-Accomplishable	-	TTPA	=	5 minutes

Characteristic Analyzed (from Team)   **Delight (100%)**

Time to place order	-	TTD	.	TTPA	-
_____	-		.		-
_____	-	B	.		-
_____	-		.		-
	-		.		-
	-		.		-
	-	A	.		-
	-		.		-
	-		.		-
	-		.		-

Satisfaction is nonexistent

matrices (i.e., one with measures/target values and one with functions), the team creates a more complete set of concepts on how to solve for the customer's problems.

The team will brainstorm these functions, based on their experience (multifunctional) with the product and customer. The knowledge gained from in-context customer visits and/or outside support from other market research helps focus the discussions.

Function attributes can be developed by visualizing and flow-charting a functional decomposition of the product and/or by describing the functions that must be performed to satisfy the customer. The DB&N team used both in developing their function list (see figure 11.4).

Figure 11.4

DB&N Product Planning Matrix for Functions

Product Planning for Functions

CORRELATIONS Legend

Strong Positive	●	9
Positive	O	3
Negative	✕	-3
Strong Negative	✳	-9

WANTS vs. MEASURES Legend

Strong	●	9
Moderate	O	3
Weak	△	1

FUNCTIONS / CUSTOMER NEEDS	Regulate material deposits	Replace mechanism	Store mechanism	Support finger pressure	Attach instrument to storage places	Fit in Hand	Deactivate marking mechanism	Contact medium	Deposit writing material	Choice Importance
Solid Feel	●	O		●		△	O	●	O	5
Easy to handle		●		O	O	●	●			10
Easy to find			△	O	●					5
Writes smoothly	●			O		△		O	△	10
Looks expensive					O		O			5
Creates good impression	●	●	●	O	O	O	△	△	O	25
Easy to order										5
Easy to replace										5
Protect the environment	O							O	O	10
Minimal trash from packaging				△	△					20
FUNCTION IMPORTANCE	390	330	230	215	185	180	145	130	130	

Maximum Value = 390.0
— FUNCTION IMPORTANCE
Minimum Value = 0.0

For the DB&N team the "regulate material deposits" function is the most important in satisfying customer needs. That is because it has the largest sum of impact relationships and choice importance values.

In both the previous matrices, the measures/functions are something the company can control. These are things that can be influenced through definition and design methods. The benefit of these matrices is to help the team understand which things take priority. This can be any part of the value delivery proposition if at the strategic level, or any function of a solution at the "product" level. It must be noted at this point that there is great flexibility in the CIDM/ QFD process, and the kind of matrices that may be completed.

Facilitators play a key role in helping teams decide the types of matrices that are needed. CIDM is an idea generation and decision-making process, and actions should be taken based on those ideas and decisions focusing on the customer. For example, the team may decide to start a project and complete more detailed measures/ function matrices. This project could explore how they will achieve the "five-minute" target value defined for the characteristic "time to place order" in figure 11.3. Depending on the ideas generated and the decisions made, an updated road map should be created to reflect the actual set of matrices completed. This updated road map should be included in reports to management (see figure 11.6).

TeamTalk Review and Reporting

An important team activity is capturing the dialogue of the team matrix during completion and analysis. For example, in figure 11.4, a significant discussion or difference of opinion may arise over the relationship strength between "replace mechanism" and "creates good impression." Usually, much rich dialogue and discovery will result from such an exchange. Facilitators and team leaders need to view these exchanges as good things and encourage "controlled conflict." This is the point at which true organizational learning occurs. To keep track of this detailed information, the TeamTalk charts would be shown on figure 11.5.

Figure 11.5

Example of DB&N TeamTalk Record and Report Dissemination

Issues / Concerns

Can one material support both "support finger pressure" and "slide in hand crook"?

Will clipping mechanisms interfere with the retract effort?

Can we make a mechanism to easily retract?

Actions

What Who When

Research materials, B. Weisman, 9/30/94

Brainstorm clipping mechanism options, B. Weisman, 9/30/94

Explore mfg. issues for the retract mechanism #2, M. Wright, 10/12/94

Ah-ha's

Patent opportunities on concepts #3 & #5

Can't make the new pyro-plastic profitably.

Report #12, 9/24/94:

The team completed the function matrix discussion and analyzed the House of Quality again. Since we resolved the most important function issues last meeting, discussion ensued on the internal mechanisms needed to support the writing instrument "retracting function."

A potential patent opportunity has presented itself on mechanism concepts #3 and #5.

We also must evaluate our manufacturing capability when it comes to Material #4 in the configuration proposed.

We will have decisions on these issues by the next regular meeting.

We also decided that a separate action-oriented function matrix will be required to respond to the needs "easy to order" and "easy to replace."

Developing a usable and applicable process for capturing and processing such team knowledge is one of the more important results of CIDM. Most companies fail to capture and use this information. For years, product development managers have been talking about preserving the corporate "knowledge base" for product development.

The TeamTalk charts are the most practical means that we have found to do just that. Managing and disseminating the information is

Figure 11.6

Updated Road Map Included with Report

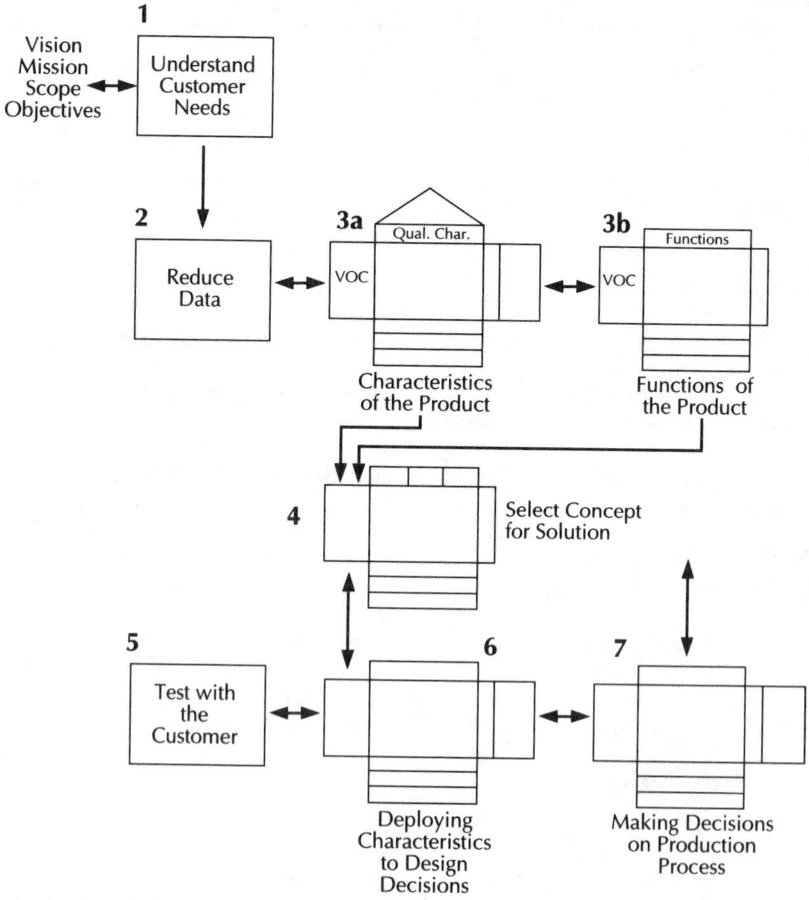

indeed a discipline. The challenge for TeamTalk is to make these data available to the right people so that they can share the understanding.

Note in figure 11.5 that recorded issues and actions are much more solution-oriented than previous TeamTalk charts. The actions list has raised specific questions on what the team must do to get proper resolution to the issues. Issues at this stage are generally more design-oriented and help form the basis for formulating solution concepts.

Note, also, that after examining the function matrix, the team realized that the customer needs, "easy to order" and "easy to replace" will require a separate type of function matrix because responding to those needs requires action-oriented functions outside the instrument itself. These are activities of the BIG P.

The following are steps for completing and reporting solution planning matrices, including the information collected using TeamTalk:

1. Record customer needs.
2. Record perception data.
3. Complete calculations of importance.
4. Develop quality characteristics and measures and/or functions.
5. Explore potential conflicts in quality characteristics.
6. Develop relationships to needs.
7. Complete calculations by multiplying the customer importance value times the strength of the relationship value and sum each column.
8. Reflect and analyze results.
9. Summarize TeamTalk charts and develop reports.

INFORMATION QUALITY AND DECISION QUALITY

One of the concepts presented in the future quality model is that of the "quality of decisions." It is our belief that this concept *is* the future of quality. The quality of decisions and the ability to adapt are supported by the approach we've been discussing in this book:

- Knowing the customers' value delivery choices.
- Creating high-energy adaptive teams (HEAT).
- Building skills in data acquisition, synthesis, and extraction.

These are the primary drivers of "decision quality." CIDM is pulling together the necessary tools and methods, using them to make decisions, and developing the requisite people skills in addressing the improvement of decision quality.

As information technology continues to evolve toward the ability to quickly provide information to individuals, the CIDM model, in our opinion, will become a cornerstone to achieving flexibility in decision-making and quality in an organization.

Formulating Alternative Product Concepts and Concept Selection

After using the product planning matrices to identify and prioritize the product variables under our control, the team is in a position to understand the issues surrounding the competing product concepts. In fact, experienced facilitators begin capturing this information throughout the previous matrix work.

A useful tool in concept selection is based upon early work by Stuart Pugh.[1] It allows the team to use the prioritized "measures" and "functions" from the previous two matrices as "decision criteria" to help formulate and select a concept. Bear in mind that this matrix, like previous ones, is merely a vehicle to guide a cross-functional team toward higher-quality decisions. It is a "team dialogue generator." Tools like the matrix, VOCT database, and TeamTalk aid the team in capturing key decision information.

Several product concepts need to be considered, as shown in the top of the sample matrix below (see figure 11.7). As the team considers each concept, in the context of the decision criteria, the "best" product concept slowly emerges.

Figure 11.7

Concept Selection Example for DB&N Team

Concept Selection

	Concept Selection Legend		BASELINE (Multi-pen Clone)	Multi-Pen Executive	Fountain Pen	Ballpoint Pen	Pencil	IMPORTANCE VALUE
	Better	+						
	Same	S						
	Worse	-						
FUNCTIONS								
Support finger pressure				+	-	-	-	215
Fit in hand				+	+	-	-	180
Attach instrument to storage places				S	-	S	S	185
Deactivate marking mechanism				+	-	-	+	145
Store mechanism				S	-	+	+	230
Replace mechanism				S	-	+	+	375
Contact medium				S	-	+	S	130
Deposit writing material				+	-	-	S	130
Regulate material deposits				S	-	S	+	390
QUALITY CHARACTERISTICS								
"Impression" Panel test				+	+	-	-	300
Amount of packaging				+	-	S	S	280
Amount recyclable material				+	-	+	+	225
"Shape & Fit" Panel test					+	-	-	160
Number of attachment modes				+	-	-	-	105
Mark application pressure				S	+	S	S	105
"Feel" Panel results				+	+	-	-	70
Time to place order				+	-	S	S	50
Material quality index				+	+	-	-	45
Time to replace				+	-	S	S	45
Total Pluses				1790	860	960	1365	
Total Minuses					2505	1350	1075	
Total Sames				1415		1055	925	
Leading Candidate				1790	-1645	-390	290	

After completing the concept selection matrix, further analysis may reveal where the "winning concept" may be weak where others are strong. Again, this is not a bad thing; it should be viewed as an opportunity to establish perhaps a stronger winning concept by combining strong features.

CONCEPT SELECTION EXAMPLE FOR DB&N TEAM

Notice where the winning concept is better(+). It is important to ask why this is so and look at the weak areas to see if some of the other solutions are strong there. Perhaps a new hybrid solution can emerge from this analysis.

Steps for Completing the Concept Selection Matrix

1. Transform measures and functions from the previous planning matrices to the left hand list.
2. Formulate concept alternatives via brainstorming.
3. Establish a baseline concept.
4. Complete linkages by asking for each measure/function: "Is this concept better than, the same as, or worse than, the baseline concept?"
5. Complete calculations by adding the pluses, and subtracting the minuses, after multiplying each by the importance value on the right side of the matrix to determine strongest concept.
6. Reflect on results and make decisions.
7. Summarize TeamTalk charts and write report.

Verifying Product Integrity and Quality Deployment

Having established the identity and priority of the key measures of our solution, the team must now deploy decisions to the key quality controls level in the organizations responsible for delivering the solution. All people "building the product" must have input in the process to deliver what the customer wants. As explained earlier in the enhanced quality model in part II, this is planning for functional quality, that which will satisfy the customer.

Once a concept has been selected, the QFD tasks now focus on the production process. This is when all of the team knowledge gained will support creativity and good judgment. Only those matrices required for decision-making need to be completed. The team needs to keep the project mission statement in mind and develop a matrix scenario needed to answer the key questions. What questions are not yet answered? Which organizational functions are the key in forming and delivering a high-quality solution? How will the solution be realized? This is the key in establishing a meaningful planning scenario for further matrix development.

THE DESIGN MATRIX

The design matrix is constructed by moving the measures from the product planning matrix to the left side and reaching consensus through brainstorming on design parameters that can be controlled by the design team. The design parameters are now "concept specific" (see figure 11.8 on page 186).

DB&N TEAM DESIGN MATRIX

Note that design parameters "mechanism stowage clearance," "enclosure tightness," and "mechanism part clearance" have strong impacts on delivering the product measure 'feel' panel test. Also note that after completing the calculations, that design parameter "auxiliary attach flatness" is most important in satisfying the measures and functions.

The design matrix helps the team focus on key elements needing attention. For example, after sorting the "design factors" by percent priority, it became apparent that the service element quality characteristics "time to order" and "time to replace" required separate planning activities to develop and deploy quality into a customer service center.

It also became apparent that additional market research was

Figure 11.8

DB&N Team Design Matrix

Design Matrix

WANTS vs. MEASURES Legend		
Strong	●	9
Moderate	○	3
Weak	△	1

DESIGN FACTORS (functions)	Ink flow rate	Lead hardness	Mechanism eject time	Mechanism stowage clearance	Case strength	Surface tackiness	Clip point clearance	Auxiliary attach flatness	Top surface smoothness	Retract mechanism force	Writing point finish	Ink drying time	Lead antismudge	DESIGN FACTORS (Measures)	Shape aspect ratio	Enclosure lightness	Material reuse factor	Roller sleeve surface finish	Mechanism part clearance	Color appeal test	Surface appeal test	IMPORTANCE VALUE
FUNCTIONS																						
Support finger pressure					●	○		○			△				○		△					215
Fit in hand					●	△	○	●							○							180
Attach instrument to storage places						○	●	●							○							185
Deactivate marking mechanism			△	○								●				△			○			145
Store mechanism			○	●							△				△	●			○			230
Replace mechanism			●	●											○	△			●			375
Contact medium											●	△	△					△	○			130
Deposit writing material	●	●									●	△	△					△	●			130
Regulate material deposits	●	●									●	○	○					△	●			390
QUALITY CHARACTERISTICS																						
"Impression" Panel test				△		△	△	●	○						●					●	●	300
Amount of packaging			○	○												●			△			280
Amount recyclable material	△	△			○	○			○			△	○	○			●	△		△	△	225
"Shape & Fit" Panel test	△			△	●			●	●	△	△				●	△		△	○			160
Number of attachment modes		△				△	○	●	△						○							105
Mark application pressure	●	●									●	△	△		○		△	○				105
"Feel" Panel test			△	●						○	△					●			△	●		70
Time to place order																						50
Material quality index	○	○			○	○			○	○												45
Time to replace																				●	●	45
Design Factor Priority	6145	5985	4365	7810	3585	5475	2460	7935	4875	1905	7600	2210	2210		7665	5900	2780	6055	5890	3330	3330	
Percent Priority	6.3	6.1	4.5	8.0	3.7	5.6	2.5	8.1	5.0	1.9	7.8	2.3	2.3		8.0	6.0	2.8	6.2	6.0	3.4	3.4	

Maximum Value = 7935.0
— Design Factor Priority
Minimum Value = 0.0

Target Value

needed to probe more deeply into customer perceptions of "shape aspect ratio" (the first design factor for "measures").

Work at this stage becomes very "design specific." The TeamTalk charts become filled with tasks and actions related to further clarifying the design and market research to help do that.

THE MANUFACTURING PROCESS MATRIX

After deploying the quality characteristics and functions to design factors, the next consideration to be made in assuring product definition integrity is the exploration of key elements of the manufacturing process that impact key design factors.

A variety of methods exist to plan the details of the "manufacturing process." Depicted in figure 11.9 is a "process matrix" example showing how the manufacturing process steps can be itemized and prioritized for specific parts once they have been identified.

In this example, the top four design factors from the design matrix form the left-hand list in the matrix. The team then develops the process factors in the top list of the matrix and explores the relationships. Summing the multiple of percent priority and relationship values helps set process planning priorities. These represent the processes that must be controlled properly to assure the "functional quality dimension."

Having a cross-functional team that includes those knowledgeable of the process of manufacturing is important.

Marilyn Liner's experience at Raychem Corporation highlights the importance of using these detailed level matrices: "In my experience, the projects using QFD that have achieved the best bottom-line results, have been those that continued using the process for manufacturing process planning and development. These subsequent charts are much easier to complete and enable more leverage to be gained from the initial QFD work."

This phase brings into focus the nuances of the production process while the product itself is being developed and designed.

Figure 11.9

DB&N Team Manufacturing Processes Matrix

Process Planning Matrix

DESIGN FACTORS	PROCESS FACTORS			Molding Capability	Automated Assembly Capability			Ball material polishing set point	Ball socket grinding tolerance				Percent Priority
Mechanism stowage clearance				●	●								8.0
Auxillary attach flatness				O	O								8.1
Writing point finish								●	O				7.8
Shape aspect ratio				●	O								8.0
Process Planning Priority				169	120			70	23				

WANTS vs. MEASURES Legend
Strong ● 9
Moderate O 3
Weak △ 1

Note that the most important process parameters are "molding capability" and "automated assembly capability." This provided the DB&N team with a direction and feeling of priority, prompting them to revisit their design concepts and begin to focus on discussions for a solution.

Steps for Completing a Manufacturing Process Matrix

1. Transform design factors from previous matrices.
2. Develop process steps and measures.
3. Develop control methods.
4. Complete calculations and set priorities.
5. Analyze results.
6. Summarize TeamTalk and reports.

Process Improvement

The final phase of the deployment cycle is continuous improvement. It is often said that QFD is one of the most misunderstood continuous improvement tools around today. There is no question that if a team begins to expect miracles from QFD while using it only as a tool set, they are begging for trouble. CIDM/QFD as a mind-set should be viewed as a process to gain forever a greater understanding of customer priorities, and therefore gain greater ability to provide what the customer will consider a "delight."

Teams that use these tools must work continuously to improve their abilities. There is no limit to making better decisions based on customer-focused data and structured analysis of information.

The Matrix Concept: Why It Works

QFD is not a miracle process in that it does not "give you the answers." It is a methodology that creates an environment for organizational learning. It provides focus and structure for people to share their knowledge and work together. It provides the framework for exploring in depth how issues interact.

Properly implemented in the CIDM structure, QFD makes possible high-quality decisions earlier in a product or service development/improvement process, when there is still time to do something about potential problems.

Figure 11.10 shows a simple matrix example. In it are three customer needs and four company responses. The relationship matrix shows which responses impact the satisfaction of each of the needs. In this simple example, response "A" has the greatest impact on satisfying everything the customer wants. It is the most important thing we can control to satisfy customers. This is the essence of the matrix; it allows a team to examine a deeper understanding of their planned responses to customers, item by item, then summarize that understanding in the form of "priorities."

In establishing the relationship connections, a cross-functional team may have differing opinions about whether or not a relationship exits, and the relative strength of those relationships. This dialogue provides deeper understanding for a team. A team that has developed the ability to create positive dialogue in establishing such relationships exhibits a major trait of what we refer to as a high-energy adaptive team (HEAT).

The name is appropriate because it requires high energy to complete these matrices properly. And it requires a certain degree of adaptability because the team must remain open to new discoveries during the process. One of the key roles of a facilitator is to create and sustain that energy in a positive learning environment during team meetings.

Figure 11.10

Simple Matrix Example

	A	B	C	D
Need 1	O	O		
Need 2	O		O	O
Need 3	O			O

There are many matrices that can be developed to complete a CIDM project. In order to get the greatest amount of benefit from latter stages of QFD, the team continually must answer the question "What do we need to understand, now, based upon the information we have?"

Therein lies the secret of CIDM/QFD: a high-energy, adaptive team working together in a positive learning environment, using the discipline and structure of the matrix tools to make good decisions early in a development process.

MATRIX ANALYSIS

It is often said that when the matrices are complete, the process of development can begin. How a team interprets the information in the matrices is key to good decision-making. A team should be careful not to "read things into" the matrices. When differences of opinion arise, they should look for opportunities for more definitive information rather than arguing over incomplete information.

Care should be taken to document decisions made as a result of team interpretations. A useful process is to have a summary section in each team's minutes to itemize key decisions. Such practice becomes natural over time and is very useful for management reports. (A useful format for matrix analysis and recording is included in appendix VI.)

CHAPTER 12

Project Management and Evaluating Project Success

The structure and logic in the matrices allow teams to focus on the key elements of quality to be developed for the customer. These "technical" elements are deployed into greater detail within the functions that form quality. Commensurate with the technical elements of quality are the management elements.

Leadership

As mentioned earlier, project success is closely tied to the quality of leadership. This relates not only to the project leader, but to all leadership as well. Leaders up and down the chain need to be aware of the CIDM/QFD efforts in order to be able to overcome barriers and facilitate the internalization of the processes.

An important attribute of project leadership is how able the team is to accept "partial successes," aka "failures." Perceived failure can be as simple as doing "less than perfect work"; this perception is often the case when dealing with fuzzy concepts in early development phases. The project leader must stress the importance of this conceptual work and move forward. Failures can also be as significant as making tactical blunders in front of a customer. The leader must anticipate these partial successes in first-time projects and keep the team motivated.

But the fundamental role of leadership is to make sure the goals, targets, product definition, and decisions generated by the QFD matrices get accomplished.

Process Execution

One measure of QFD success is completing the process. In initial projects, there is ample opportunity for the project to be discontinued from a variety of sources. Niccolò Machiavelli in *The Prince* describes the challenges faced by "reformers": "Thus it arises that on every opportunity for attacking the reformer, his opponents do so with the zeal of partisans, the others only defend him half-heartedly, so that between them he runs great danger."

The reformer's challenge then is to create "a new order of things." Project leadership faces such challenges in internalizing CIDM.

In this environment, achieving project milestones is a measure of success. Another measure is the time a team takes to analyze the data and develop conclusions that have a feel of confidence. The CIDM process supports the deployment of the decisions through a two-way process known as "catchball."

THE CIDM STRATEGY ACTION DEPLOYMENT PROCESS

Figure 12.1 shows the flow of the strategy deployment process. The QFD priorities, targets, and actions are linked to the strategy deployment forms (SDF) and an "owner" assigned to each one. The owner most probably will be from outside the QFD project team.

The key to the process is that management and the action team responsible for achieving the targets "negotiate" the timing and the expectations of the targets themselves. This process is indicated by the double arrows in figure 12.1. Sometimes, for whatever reason, the action team finds that the current conditions dictate that the target cannot be met. Catchball is used to manage the improvement process and to get the resources required to be able to achieve the target values of the actions required.

Figure 12.1

CIDM Strategy Deployment Process

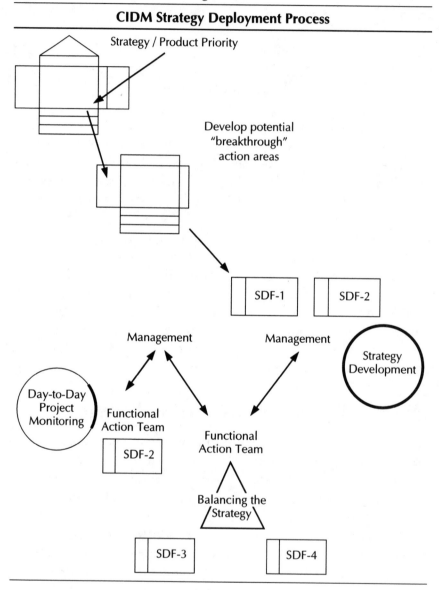

The Management Forms

The purpose of the forms is as follows:

SDF-1: Assigns an owner to high-priority actions.

SDF-2: Relates the action target to available resources.

SDF-3: Tracks and manages performance.

SDF-4: Manages continuous improvement.

To demonstrate the management of the forms, figure 12.2 indicates how the focus on external customers with a balance of focus on internal priority and strategy converge in the CA-PDCA (Check-Act-Plan-Do-Check-Act) cycle. This figure graphically describes CIDM from a continuously improving management perspective. It describes the key elements to be monitored in practicing and achieving adaptive leadership.

Figure 12.2

Continuous Improvement to Meet Targets

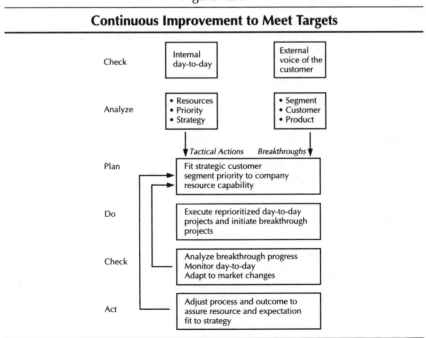

Summary of the CIDM/QFD Process

Overall, the CIDM process can be described in phases or stages:

Phase 1. Strategy and target development.

Phase 2. The strategy deployment process.

Phase 3. Day-to-day project management.

These phases, properly executed, link the company objectives and strategies to the customer needs, then link the objectives and strategies to the final solution definition and the internal company processes. The outcome is that all activities are aligned and working together.

PHASE 1. STRATEGY AND TARGET DEVELOPMENT

Phase 1 involves an ongoing cycle of the following tasks:

- Mission, scope, and objective definition and team agreement.
- Segment and customer identification.
- Customer knowledge acquisition.
- Understanding of the customers' "choice" perceptions surrounding their "wants and needs" and the ability of our company and the competition to provide them.
- Team analyses of the data and translation of customer "knowledge" to team "understanding and priority" of target values.

Responsibilities are assigned as follows:

Senior Management (President, Vice Presidents)

1. Using the CIDM/QFD process, the management team will identify the value delivery objectives and strategies, i.e., the operational action objectives, and the priorities leading to strategies. This will be a high-level understanding of the customers' perception of

the company's "value delivery proposition." After developing an understanding of the customers' "choice-based" buying importance and the customers' perceptions of the competition, the team will prioritize the data to identify the top measures to develop a "strategic value delivery" and/or "product differentiation proposition." These action items will, in effect, set strategic directions for the company teams, which then detail the activities that will assure competitive differentiation.

2. Output: The strategy action recommendations from this top-level effort are referred to as the "management product."

PHASE 2. DAY-TO-DAY PROJECT MANAGEMENT

Senior Management

1. The management team will, as required, or at least quarterly, analyze a high level status report acquired from throughout the company to understand the balance of resources and projects. The outcome is to prioritize the projects as they relate to the current market targets.

2. Output: A high-level list of projects and their priority for "direct" and "indirect customer impact." This process allows the management team to evaluate the projects as to their effect on current customer-linked priorities and markets. This effort will determine needs for additional resources and/or the need to redistribute resources among projects.

Managers

1. The department level managers will keep a running log of projects and resource allocation. This log will also show movement of resources that directly and indirectly affect the customer.

2. Output: The process allows the managers to interact with senior management in a "catchball process." This allows for balance of the department/company resources and the customer and segment market changes, as required.

PHASE 3. THE STRATEGY DEPLOYMENT PROCESS

Senior Management

1. The senior management team will make strategy and action decisions. They can utilize data from the "management product" (strategy "House of Quality") or other means such as the day-to-day studies (documented in SDF forms), segmentation studies, customer choice studies, corporate strategy directives, among others, to arrive at final decisions on "breakthrough" strategic action goals and objectives.

2. These will be documented in form SDF-1 and distributed to the manager and/or action team leader.

Manager and/or Action Team Leader

1. The responsible person will follow one of a number of action paths:
   A. Review the goal and/or objective to determine the next action and then assign the action to other teams.
   B. Define a multifunctional team to evaluate the goal and/or objective, using tools like CIDM at the project/product level or an action team to define the project and execute the plan.

In the case of "A," usually internal projects affecting company customers, the project team would define a project and interactively "catchball" with management to get agreement on the scope and timing of the project. The team would use the SDF-3 and SDF-4 forms to document and control deviations to this project plan.

In the case of "B," usually directly driven by the customer and directly documented by a QFD House, the team would develop a multifunctional team to define and execute a CIDM/QFD project into action in an effort to get more detailed direct customer input. The team would use SDF-3 and SDF-4 forms to interactively "catchball" with the management team based on the "binding limits" defined by senior management.

Action Teams

1. These teams will use SDF-4 forms to report deviations to the plan in an interactive mode with management.

CHAPTER 13

Summary: The Future of CIDM

The customer-integrated decision-making (CIDM) approach to QFD described in our book is a powerful, proven methodology for decision-making. It is a way to focus teams of people on critical elements in a product development process so that quality is designed into a product. Product, in this context, is defined broadly as anything being delivered to customers. CIDM/QFD provides a structure by which information in the form of needs statements of customers can be translated into meaningful information to guide the product development process. This structure examines the details of how the customers' many wants and needs get translated into design features of the product as well as parameters in the many processes that work together to develop the product. CIDM/QFD is about paying attention to those details early in the development efforts so that quality is designed into the product-process system.

CIDM/QFD DEALS WITH VARIABLE DATA IN A COMPETITIVE WORLD

In any development process, we are always faced with uncertainty and risk. This comes about from the realization that customers' needs change with time. Even though customers' basic needs are relatively stable, their priorities of what is important to them change more frequently. When these needs are expressed as data, we must realize that the data vary with time.

What does the customer need? What does the customer think about our product? What does the customer think about the competition's product? What does it take to satisfy the customer at any given point in time? QFD allows us to analyze rigorously these questions in the context of what it means to us in our development efforts.

CIDM/QFD IS A WAY OF DEALING WITH UNKNOWNS

As we gain a higher degree of clarity about customer needs, we also realize a lot about what we don't know.

Figure 13.1 represents two competing solution realization processes and their representative knowledge about a customer's usage environment. "XX" represents knowledge that we share with our competitor; "!!!" represents knowledge we have about our customer, but the competition does not; "??" represents knowledge that our competitor has about the customer, but we don't have; and "YY" represents knowledge we all have. As the knowns and unknowns become evident over time, CIDM/QFD provides focus for our future efforts to clarify and discover what we don't know, as well as solidify in our minds where the opportunities might be in a competitive market place.

Figure 13.1

CIDM/QFD Helps Reveal New Views
of Our Customers' Competitive World

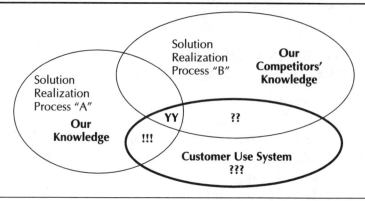

CIDM/QFD IS A WAY OF DEALING WITH FUZZY INFORMATION

Because CIDM/QFD uses a systems view of product development that is very structured, we find it easier to deal with information that initially is quite fuzzy. CIDM/QFD's translation of needs into a context for our development efforts allows us to take actions to clarify fuzzy information.

CIDM/QFD IS PROACTIVE DECISION-MAKING

CIDM/QFD structures information in the form of matrices and tables early in the development process. Issues for clarification can be raised in time for us to do something about them. The structure allows us to see the implications of our decisions before we make them, which, of course, makes the decisions much easier. We therefore make better decisions early, well in advance of product introduction.

CIDM/QFD IS EXPLORING RELATIONSHIPS AND THEIR INFLUENCE

One of the tools used extensively in CIDM/QFD is the matrix, sometimes referred to simply as "quality charts."[1] The matrix allows us to explore the influences that elements in our product process have on one another. The matrix allows us to examine the many-to-many relationships that drive out relative importances.

The number and types of charts used, and what information goes into each chart, depend entirely on the application. How the charts tie together, and how many levels of detail are explored, are matters of design. The logic and structure of the assembled charts provide a rich, robust information environment for examining and understanding the influence of relationships on decision-making.

CIDM/QFD IS TEAM-THINKING ABOUT THE WHOLE

When CIDM/QFD charts are developed and used by a team of people representing all functions in the product process, a powerful context emerges for deeper understanding and meaning of critical design and development issues. The ability of teams to work together becomes very important; team members must spend the time needed to explore the details in the CIDM/QFD chart so that cross-functional understanding emerges to avoid mistakes downstream.

All functions play a role in the development effort. By examining the systems view of the product process, which is represented by the assembled matrices and tables, all functions can begin to see the impact of their part. A rich context emerges for optimization of the whole.

CIDM/QFD IS ABOUT SWEAT!

In product development, we have a choice. We can sweat the details early, or we can sweat them later. Make no mistake about it, there is a lot of work in gathering, assembling, discussing, and structuring the data that CIDM/QFD requires. But the data are critical decision data. By paying attention early, we avoid costly errors later. The comfort and clarity of knowing details early streamline subsequent processes.

CIDM/QFD IS AN INFORMATION ARCHITECTURE FOR VALUE DELIVERY DECISION-MAKING

In summary, CIDM/QFD provides the information architecture within which teams involved in product development can make decisions. Any value delivery process is extremely complex. CIDM/QFD helps structure critical data so that their influences on each other can be examined and decisions made early to deliver quality to the customer.

Appendices

The DB&N Example Storyboard

The figures used throughout this book tell a story. Selected figures from part III have been assembled in this appendix for your convenience in reading to help solidify your understanding of deploying the customer data within the CIDM process. It is hoped that this storyboard will be used for learning CIDM principles, and not rotely copied in hopes for success in your own organization. Adapting the principles to your environment is the real key.

Figure 7.2 The BIG P

With the vision of the new product, in this case an executive writing instrument, the team wants to make sure that they take the complete product picture into account and not get too focused on any particular solution too early.

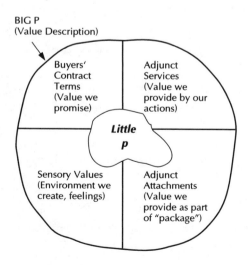

Figure 7.3 Mission

A mission statement is developed to align the team.

1. *Name*   The mission of the DB&N Corporate New Products Team
2. *Activity*   is to design, develop, and implement
3. *Product*   a new and improved executive writing instrument
4. *Rationale*   which will allow us to penetrate the high-end market.

Figure 7.4 Scope

A scope statement is developed to bound the activity.

The new product will encompass the executive writing instrument category for the U.S. and Canadian markets and will help penetrate the (high-end) users' market. It will be developed using rapid-prototyping techniques, leveraging what we have learned from launching products in Europe. The development budget is in the six-figure range and the product should support a family of products spanning three to five years in useful life. Although the product is new, its technology is not anticipated to be revolutionary. We will rely on existing, proven core technology and methods.

Figure 7.5 Objectives

Specific objectives are agreed upon based upon management guidelines. This assures that the aim for the CIDM system is understood by all.

In developing and delivering the new writing instrument, we will achieve the following objectives:

1. *Provide differentiation in the executive segment.*
2. *Focus on the U.S. and Canadian executive market.*
3. *Utilize current production capability.*

Figure 7.6 Road Map

With the help of the team facilitator, a map is constructed of the planning documents to be created during the CIDM activity.

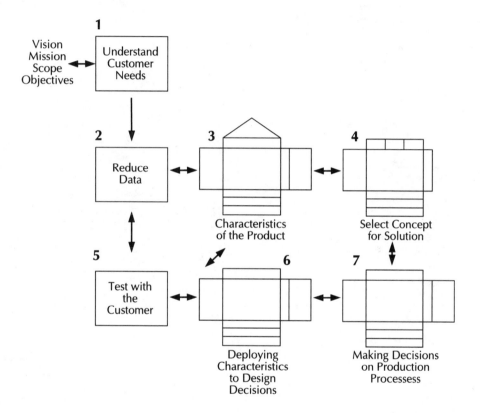

Figure 7.7 Project Plan

From the road map, a detailed project plan is developed.

```
Vision, Mission,
Scope, Objectives        /------/

Understand
customer needs           /--------------------/

Reduce data                   /-------/

Translate the VOC into
product characteristics            /-----------/

Formulate and select
best solution concept                /------/

Test with the customer               /-----/

Deploy characteristics
to design decisions                    /------/

Make decisions on
production processes                     /-----/

Continuously improve
the solution and
development processes     /-------------------------------/
                             Time ──➤
```

Figure 8.1 Team

With things clear on what needs to be accomplished, the final team roster is developed.

Core Team

Team leader	Ms. Smith
Design	Mr. Weisman
Marketing	Mr. Marks
Manufacturing	Ms. Wright
Sales	Mr. Jansen
Internal Facilitator	Mr. Dent
External Facilitator	Mr. Barnard

Extended Team 1 (Technology)

R&D	Mr. Ernst
Plant 2	Mr. Block
Lab	Mr. Hale
Purchasing	Ms. Gray

Extended Team 2 (Sales)

Sales Manager	Mr. Jansen
Region 1	Mr. Carl
Region 2	Mr. Springer
Region 3	Ms. Dumas

Figure 8.2 TeamTalk Charts

During these initial meetings, team concerns are captured using TeamTalk charts. This helps them to assure clear next steps and keeps the team from getting bogged down on longer-term issues. Significant learnings are documented for future reference.

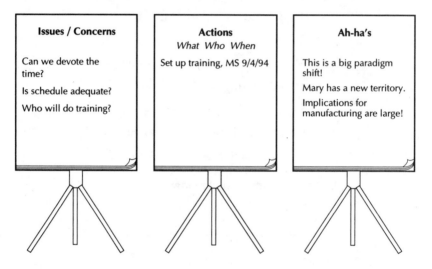

Issues / Concerns	Actions What Who When	Ah-ha's
Can we devote the time? Is schedule adequate? Who will do training?	Set up training, MS 9/4/94	This is a big paradigm shift! Mary has a new territory. Implications for manufacturing are large!

Figure 8.3 Communications Plan

A team plan for communicating during the project is developed and agreed to. This assures that the flow of decision information is not delayed or misinterpreted.

Meeting agendas will be published ahead of time.
The team will rotate the recording of the minutes.
Jim Smith will approve minutes.
Bob Marks will distribute the minutes via e-mail.
We will keep a project activity plan in the war room.
Information will be updated weekly.
Team meetings will be from 8 to 12 each Tuesday.
Remote team members will participate via conference calls.

Figure 9.1 Segmentation

With the plan and team in place, a rigorous segmentation process results in a cascade diagram that shows the segment the team will pursue. This raises the confidence level of profitability at the start.

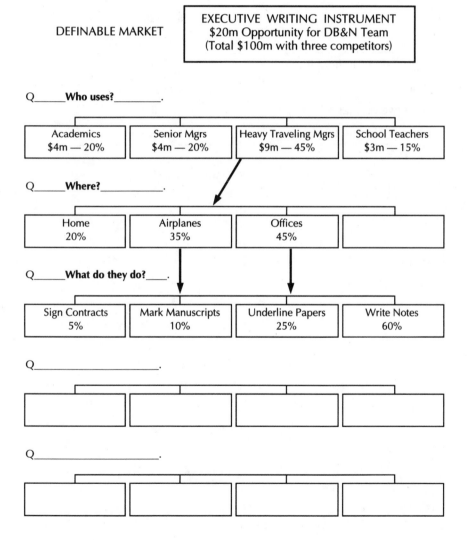

| DEFINABLE MARKET | EXECUTIVE WRITING INSTRUMENT $20m Opportunity for DB&N Team (Total $100m with three competitors) |

Figure 9.2 Customer Matrix

Within that segment, the different types of customers are identified to which attention must be devoted. This begins the process of understanding the value delivery proposition.

	SEGMENT 1
	Executives Who Do Heavy Travel
Distribution Channel Buyer	Sell To
Shopkeeper	Understand
Executive on plane	Sell To
Executive in office	Influence

Figure 9.3 VOVT

With this initial understanding, the team generates its first customer contact via the VOVT. Much information and many questions emerge as a result.

				$1,000 Test		
Name:						
Title:						
Company:						
I Want . . .	$100 Test	PENTEL	EAGLE	DB&N	( )	( )
Training						
Frequent writing seminars						
Needs no training to use						
Support						
Be able to buy anywhere						
Repair centers						
Immediate replacement						
Commercial Issues						
Easy to manipulate and use						
High image value						
Creates lasting image						
Adds to executive prestige						
Hassle free warranty returns						
Beautiful operation and feel						
Cost						
Reasonable price						
Unlimited warranty						
Quality						
Will last forever						
Feels solid						
Never fails						

Figure 10.1 Interview Guide

From the initial customer contact, questions are formulated for use in the "open-ended" in-context customer visits.

Check-in: (opening the interview)

Hello, thank you for giving us your time today. As we mentioned on the phone, we are interested in better understanding your wants and needs concerning the writing instruments you use. We will use this information combined with the results of several other interviews to better create a solution for your writing needs. With that in mind, please say what is on your mind regarding your needs in this area. All that we discuss will be kept confidential. It will be used only by our development team.

Main Body and Probe

1. *What are the problems related to writing that you face in completing your daily work?*
2. *What are the issues you deal with today in using your current writing instruments?*

Probing and Backup Questions

3. *What problems do you face using writing instruments while traveling?*
4. *Are there any other needs you might have?*
5. *What comes to mind when you think about the experience of purchasing your next writing instrument?*

Check-out: (closing the visit)

1. *Are there any topics that we should have discussed that we didn't?*
2. *I will probably have to recontact you regarding some of the things we talked about today.*
    When would be the best time to call?
    Any times that we shouldn't call?
    What number is best to reach you on?
3. *We will also be contacting you to understand the importance of the needs we discover.*

Thank you very much for your time. We will be in touch.

Figure 10.5 Affinity Tree

To synthesize and organize the customer needs statements, an affinity diagram results in a visual map of the customers' needs.

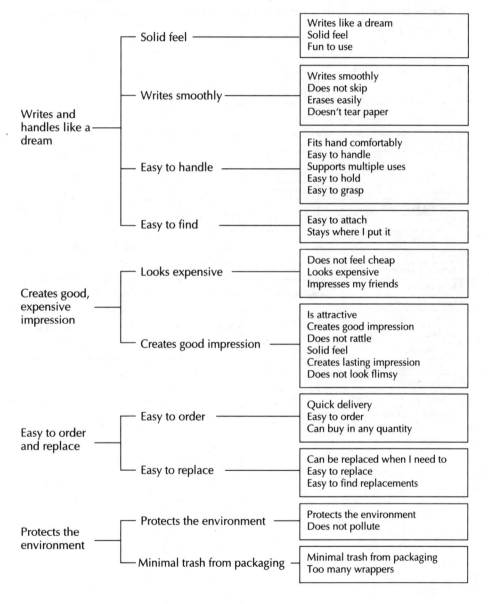

Figure 10.6 $100/$1,000 Test

Customers' choice behavior is then understood by conducting a survey using the $100/$1,000 test on the secondary level of the needs tree. This helps prioritize the list of needs based upon customers' choices.

				$1,000 Test			
Name:							
Title:							
Company:							
I Want . . .	$100 Test	PENTEL	EAGLE	DB&N	(Seiko)	(	)
Writing Function							
Solid feel	5	100					
Easy to handle	10		50				
Easy to find	5		50				
Writes smoothly	10	100					
Impression							
Looks expensive	5	100	50				
Creates good impression	25	100			200		
Ordering/Procuring							
Easy to order	5			50			
Easy to replace	5			50			
Environment							
Protects the environment	10		50				
Minimal trash from packaging	20		100				

Figure 11.1 Deployment Model

After the needs are gathered and prioritized, the team steps away from the process to reflect on how they will "deploy" the information into their organization.

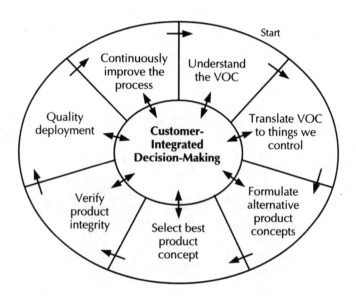

Figure 11.2 Product Planning

The needs are translated into product measures by the House of Quality (HOQ) matrix. Much rich dialogue is captured during this process because the matrix explores the relationships among items, not just the items.

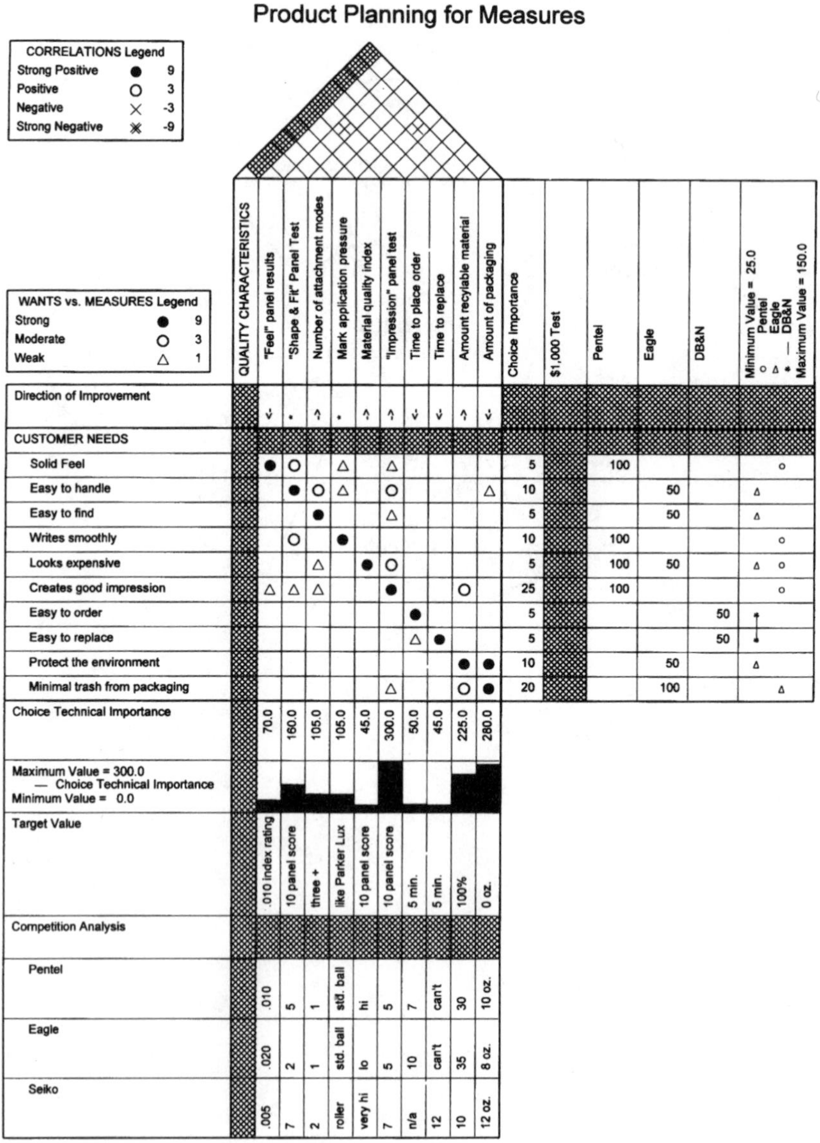

Product Planning for Measures

The Rules of Dialogue

Our rules of dialogue are based on our own experiences in adapting some of the principles of dialogue as expressed by Dr. David Bohm in a pamphlet, *On Dialogue,* available from Pegasus Communications of Cambridge, Massachusetts.

Rule #1. All participants should express their current understanding and their opinion.

Rule #2. Start the meeting by talking about how the "rules of dialogue" work.

Rule #3. Suspend assumptions and opinions (to us, this means to express your opinions and assumptions, but don't try to sell them; rather "suspend" them and understand how they relate to others').

Rule #4. Listen carefully to what others are saying and focus on trying to understand what they mean.

Rule #5. Be serious

Rule #6. Give space to others as they talk.

Rule #7. Develop a sensitivity to knowing when to talk.

Rule #8. Weigh what you want to say in your mind, and let your expressions emerge as you talk.

Rule #9. Try to see the meaning of your assumptions as they relate to the ideas of others.

These rules are fairly fundamental. We couple this process with other tools like mind-mapping and TeamTalk charts to capture the relations between ideas for documentation purposes.

High-Energy Adaptive Teams (HEAT)

The company's goal is to become a dynamic network of high-energy adaptive teams. Our experience has shown that the CIDM process, properly supported, will create these teams. High-energy and adaptive teams are the result of continuing CIDM implementations. The value of these teams does not happen by edict; it happens through effort. HEAT must start with the proper attitude.

There are varying levels of these teams. The level of value depends on the contribution of three attributes:

Energy level.

Adaptability.

Team spirit.

If any one of these attributes is missing, you will not be able to reach the high-energy level or the adaptability level that would be possible.

Energy Level

Team energy level is the capacity to do work. Energy can be reduced in teams that have individuals who are negative thinkers or are mean-spirited. Such team members often have agendas that are counter to the team mission. This behavior tends to create an environment that focuses on the "dark side" rather than the positive side of the task at hand. Energy is built in teams that are having fun; it builds through the synergy of interaction that is focused on the customer. Becoming involved "in-context" with the customer will allow discoveries to be made, and then, by reflecting on the concepts and options, all team members will develop synergy.

"High energy" in HEAT implies a higher capacity to accomplish positive work impacting the team mission. High energy allows problems to be seen as opportunities and allows quick recovery from temporary setbacks. A positive attitude is a key element in building a high team energy level.

Adaptability

The extent to which a team can adjust flexibly to the market realities surrounding it is a key characteristic of teams that have internalized adaptability. A key ingredient in maintaining adaptability is to keep an open mind to possibilities. We call this a "discovery mentality," as opposed to a "solution mentality." Unfortunately, our Western culture creates an environment in which problem solution and reacting with answers are rewarded. But the power developed from first identifying and clarifying the problem *before* jumping to a solution is the secret to maintaining a team capacity to adapt.

In battle, knowing about and planning for "possibilities" can indeed save lives. Adapting quickly to the situation at hand depends on how well the team is prepared and how open-minded. This is the attitude that is needed to maintain an "adaptive" mentality.

Team Spirit

In the beginning of a CIDM project, when a work group is formed, "team spirit" means a willingness to adhere to certain team rules and cooperating to achieve the group aim. Over time, however, the supporting influence of energy and adaptability will positively affect the spirit. It's a natural bonding process not uncommon in human nature. Respect is formed, "like" or "dislike" evolves to understanding and a respect for differences emerges.

At some point, an understanding is reached on who the team members are, what they know, and what value they are adding. There will evolve an understanding and appreciation for personal differences and ability levels. Team spirit is what keeps the group objectives at the forefront in spite of personal differences. Over time, the "team" starts to have a life of its own. The main role of the CIDM facilitator and the project leader is to keep the spirit alive. This will be done by their being perceptive enough to "latch on to" the elements of that spirit and build a team identity.

The team spirit is the soul of the team. It gives the team a morality and a reason to live. This spirit defines the bonds that tie the team together in spite of difficulties.

HEAT Core Values

1. Be truthful and honest in our efforts.
2. Have a continuous improvement process focus.
3. Explore and validate facts before making decisions.
4. Balance dialogue skills.
   Listening
   Reflecting
   Contributing

We have found that true teaming (HEAT) evolves over time. Like any coach, we've had some really good teams, some okay teams, and some teams that just didn't click. Focusing on the four values above will, in time, create a value system that allows the value of these teams to emerge. The CIDM process creates the environment for this to happen.

The Interview Guide

The interview guide is just that, a guide. It should not be thought of as a script to be read verbatim during the interview. Instead, use the detail that exists in the interview questions to rehearse and practice so that the in-context dialogue can evolve naturally during the interview. The interview guide structure can be thought of as two sections and a wrap-up, with a good opening and closing.

Interview Guide Structure

MAIN SECTION

1. What barriers do you face in doing your job as ————?

2. What issues do you encounter when dealing with ————?

3. What are the main issues as they relate to your environment?

PROBING—BACKUP AND FOCUS QUESTIONS

1. Tell us about your job.

2. (Use the understanding you have gained from the VOVT to add specific focus to your probing.)

3. In your ideal world, what would you improve over and above your current situation?

WRAP-UP SECTION

1. Wrap-up (May we call you again? When? Phone number? Best time?).

Use the probing questions you already have in your guide in each of these general categories..

Probing: Ways to Ask "Why?"

Probing is a method to get at the deeper understanding of customers' needs and wants. Think of it as an opportunity to help the customer express and verbalize his or her needs and wants clearly, rich in context and example. Some techniques that can be used in addition to asking "Why?" include:

1. Restate the customer's words. Let him listen to them so they can clarify any ambiguity.
2. Ask "Why is that true?"
3. Use phrases like "Tell me about that" or "Give me an example."
4. Use what, how, or why words in front of questions.
5. Use words to summarize by saying, "So, you're interested in reducing . . . improving . . . etc."

The goal is to get them to describe their conditions using adjectives, adverbs, and modifying phrases. *You are a detective; find out their motives!*

Customers Say the Darnedest Things . . .

People naturally talk about problems and solutions. We are interested in the underlying reasons for the problems they have or why they want certain solutions. To help with our analysis of the interviews, we will later arrange the data extracted from the interview transcripts and notes and create a database or table. We could use the following column headings in this table: Individual Type, Customer Need, Metric, Solution Expressed, Stated Problem, Related Context.

We should keep records to allow us to trace a comment back to the interview and recall the individual to do more clarification later.

APPENDIX V

Starting a User Group

Things to Consider

A success formula for starting a user group defines five major components:

1. *Localization.* Keep travel cost down, keep participation consistent, and breed a familiarity factor to help with group identity and sense of community. Allow groups to focus more on industries and applications closer to home.

2. *Open atmosphere* promotes a sense of sharing and exploration. This breeds a positive and healthy competitive environment and adds significantly to the quality of information exchanged and the value realized by each participant. We will never be able to share strategic information using case studies, but the striving for a sense of openness coupled with localized sharing will maximize information exchange.

3. *User-Driven.* Any hint of a sales focus will compromise the intent of the group. This can be especially difficult if vendors and consultants are a part of the group. Champions from industry, applying the tools in real environments, are key in developing the loyal following required to keep the group focused. We have found that, properly handled, even vendors and consultants can share their application cases.

4. *Specialization* is important to get people within the membership focused on specific issues surrounding QFD. Special interest

groups (SIG) can be developed using brainstorming techniques. Use a questionnaire to reveal identifiable interests. Then use techniques like affinity diagramming to group the data to develop the SIGs. This then provides agenda topics for future meetings. It also allows the group to focus on issues that are particularly important to them. Practical and useful case studies result from specialization.

5. *Low overhead* is a key success factor. Being able to get together quickly, disseminate information quickly, change according to rapidly evolving issues, needs, or technologies becomes important. Use fax and phone to schedule meetings. Focus on the content of discussions and information exchange, not on "high production value" of documents. E-mail is a rapidly growing method.

How to Make It Happen and Keep It Going

Someone has to take the lead, be the champion, the catalyst, the initiator, to get things going. Good "content" meetings are not so important initially as a meeting with the right spirit. Continuous improvement is a key element of an ongoing user group activity.

User-selected special interests are important in getting support and assuring that the needs of the participants are being addressed. If the SIGs are appropriate, important issues will be addressed and participation will continue. Group leadership should stay attuned to changing user interests and start new SIGs as appropriate.

Sponsors can "host" meetings to help keep costs down. Hosts can be catalysts, but care must be taken to assure that they don't become dominating forces and prohibit free expression. There is no reason why the user group concept can't be implemented by a single organization, but danger exists in missing new ideas from the outside.

User group management issues must be addressed. Will the group be formal or informal? What will be its central theme, its character, its identity? Try and stop short of adopting *Robert's Rules of Order.* A better rule of thumb is to use good meeting conduct guidelines: Have an agenda, assure group participation, be courteous, and publish minutes, even if they are handwritten.

Meeting Frequency

The frequency of meetings should be decided according to the members' needs and their ability to participate. There is a "happy medium" between "being able to work it into their schedules" and "spending so much time on this that my boss is beginning to become upset." A "rule of thumb" seems to be that meeting one day each quarter is best. The jury is still out on whether more frequent half-day sessions are better.

If enough people "pitch in" and tasks are divided with an emphasis on keeping overhead costs—both in time and dollars—low and quality of information high, frequency of meetings should not be a problem.

The BAUG: A Case Study

The San Francisco Bay Area QFD User Group was started in 1991 by Rick Norman, Doug Daetz, and a small group of California companies practicing QFD. It is a collaboration among local company representatives and consultants who meet to learn from each other through sharing ideas and experiences. The group provides an open forum for discussing and promoting the use, advancement, and improvement of the many applications of QFD and, lately, CIDM. More broadly, the BAUG is dedicated to identifying and removing barriers to the successful use of structured planning and decision-making methods in complex environments.

The first BAUG members formed several special interest groups (SIGs) around areas where they were encountering difficulties implementing QFD in their companies. The authors, members of the

QFD Input Information SIG, joined together with other BAUG members to address the need for teams using CIDM/QFD to get off on the right foot. Common problems included teams brainstorming customer needs instead of visiting customers, and management developing unrealistic expectations about what QFD could deliver.

The BAUG has evolved to a powerful dialogue group that has a simple agenda for each meeting:

Check-in.

Peer coaching.

Check-out.

The agenda is very open and unstructured. We have had some very informative and rewarding exchanges of practitioners' war stories.

The BAUG meets regularly in the Bay Area, and minutes of their meetings can be received via e-mail. (Check the Resource Guide in the back of this book on how to contact them.)

The Project Completion Tool Kit

The completion effort involves the following steps:

1. Completing the Matrices.
2. Checking and agreeing on the data in the Matrix.
3. Agreeing on the validity of the data.
   List any areas of concerns.
   Make decisions on any "shortfalls."
4. Rank the customer and characteristic importance data.
5. Make a selection on the characteristics to be analyzed and/or actioned in next steps.
   Analyzed.
      Refine data.
         Target values.
         Data with confidence concerns.
      Deployed to next phases.
   Actioned.
      Problem areas.
      Immediate opportunity issues.
6. Write, present, and distribute the final report.

Decision Flow Chart

Figure App. VI-a

Project Completion Process

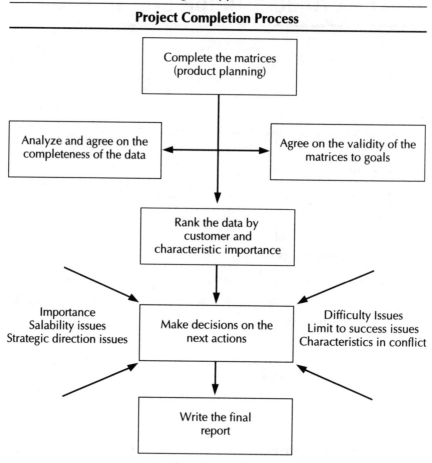

Considerations in Analyzing the Data (Product Planning)

TeamTalk charts should be used throughout to record issues, actions and Ah-ha's discovered during the following analysis.

- Comparison of *importance* ranks:
  Choice-based importance (ranked by the customer).
  Satisfaction-based importance (technical targets to hit for satisfaction).

What conclusions can we draw from examining these relative importances?
What is the stated project direction?

- Any points identifying *areas of opportunity or leverage*:
  Improvement opportunities related to:
  What should we do if—

  - A need or want is important to the customer and our competitor is significantly better than we are in the customer's mind.

  - A need is not important, but a competitor is significantly better.

  - There is an important need or want that exists and *no one* is seen as doing well in supplying a solution.

  - A need is not important and no one is seen as supplying a solution.

  - Issues related to *corporate strategic directions*:
    What should we do if:
    Issue: No strategy exists today to provide value in this area.
    Issue: The corporate strategy doesn't provide any of the needed support for the "want or need" or "characteristic."

- Issues that are discovered regarding *degrees of difficulty*:
  What should we do if:
  We find difficulty in providing:
  The characteristic itself.
  The "target value."
- Characteristics that have negative correlations between them (actions based upon analysis of the roof):

Operative question: "As we work to hit the target value of this characteristic, does it have an impact in our hitting this target value?"

  Then ask: "Is it a positive or a negative impact?"

  Then ask: "Are there any issues or opportunities?"

  Then ask: "What actions are required of us?"

- Areas that are "limits to success":
  Through analysis of the matrix by considering the issues above, what major hurdles do we face?
  Internal to the company
  Policy
  Resource
  Acquisition of knowledge
  Procedure
  Process changes required
  External to the company
  Regulatory Issue
  Technology availability

We need to make sure we define those decisions that are supported by QFD and those that are not. We need to make sure that if we do not base some of our decisions on the factors coming from QFD, we do not indicate that QFD helped us make the decision. This will help us to better understand how QFD should integrate into our overall CIDM process and other corporate processes.

Similar analysis should be done appropriately for other matrices.

Report Development

The project needs to be summarized and reported.
The following graphic describes the process to be followed:

Figure App. VI-b

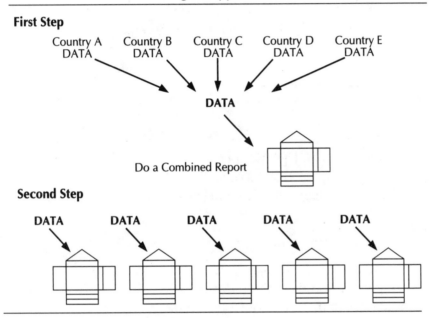

The following is a useful Table of Contents for a project completion report. It captures the essence of the project in an executive summary, and then includes sections of supporting project data. This report becomes a powerful reference for the whole company as well. It becomes the means for developing a corporate knowledge base.

Table of Contents

Secondary Research
VOVT
Customer Interview
Data Reduction

QFD Matrices
Final Charts
Overall
Country

Matrix Analysis

Overall Conclusions
Top Wants/Needs
Top Characteristic
Country Conclusions
Top Wants/Needs
Top Characteristic

Recommendations for Next Steps

Conclusions

Ah-ha's

Knowledge Provided to the:

Standard Product Development Process

Decisions on Immediate Actions

Decisions on Difficult Actions

Decisions on High-Risk Actions

Strategy Deployment Forms

These forms are used in the catchball process to deploy strategic targets.

SDF-1

Management Product Decisions		Date	For Year
Key Customer Measure ("How") by Rank		*Target Value as of This date*	*Management Assigned Owner*
_____		_____	_____
_____		_____	_____
_____		_____	_____
_____		_____	_____
Associated Customer "Wants"	*Relationships*	*Competitive Data*	
		Us _____ _____ _____ _____	
_____	_____	_____ _____ _____ _____	
_____	_____	_____ _____ _____ _____	
_____	_____	_____ _____ _____ _____	

SDF-2

Day-to-Day / Project Analyses Form		Date For Year	
Current Objectives	Priorities	Estimate of Resource to Complete	Balance Available
External			
Internal			

SDF-3

Strategy Breakthrough Performance Tracking Form				Date
Key Priority Customer Measure ("How") Identified – Target Value as of This Date –				
Supporting Action to Accomplish	Performance Measure	Target Limits	Review Period	Owner

SDF-4

Strategy Breakthrough Deviation Report Form	Date
Key Priority Customer Measure ("How") Identified – Target Value as of This Date –	
Supporting Action to Accomplish	
Issue	
Situation that existed when deviation occured Date	
Cause - method used to determine	
Short term solution in force	
Plan to assure that the problem will not recur	
Result of the solution	
Other issues as a result of this problem	

CIDM Project Facilitation and Activity List

This list is used by team leaders, facilitators, and sponsors to plan the initial CIDM/QFD effort. Actual times vary depending on scope.

Phase 1. Project Activity Checklist

Objective: Development of Benefit Characteristics and Measurements

Action: Customer requirements are translated into measurable actions in the companies' own language

Project Name _____ Location _____ Start Date _____

Barnard-Norman Associates Training and Facilitation Days

Executive Visit Day	1 Day	Date Planned ____
Preassessment Customer/Mission Day	1 Day	Date Planned ____
Segmentation Support	1 Day (optional)	Date Planned ____
Market Research and Interview Guide Development	1 Day	Date Planned ____

245

Interview Skills Overview and Practice	1 Day	Date Planned _____
QFD Tools Training	2 Days	Date Planned _____
QFD Facilitation	7/8 Days	See Team Activities dates that follow.
Off-site Support	1 Day	

   Reduce—The Data Acquired—WANTS

   Develop—The Measures for the WANTS

   Develop—Relationships (team rate of 100 hr.)

   Acquire—"Choice" Importance and Competitive Perception Data

   Analyze—Finalize the Matrix, Calculate, and Write Project Report

Project Team Activities

Complete—Precustomer Visit Work—Voice of Value Table Completion

10 Working Days Estimated   Start Date _____   Days Actual _____

Acquire—Customer Visit Data

20 Working Days Estimated   Start Date _____   Days Actual _____
                             On-Site Facilitation Date _____

Acquire—"Choice" Importance and Competitive Perception Data

10 Working Days Estimated   Start Date _____   Days Actual _____
                             On-Site Facilitation Date _____

Reduce—The Data Acquired—WANTS

8/10 Working Days Estimated   Start Date _____   Days Actual _____
                               On-Site Facilitation Date _____

Develop—The Measures for the WANTS

5/8 Working Days Estimated   Start Date _____   Days Actual _____
                              On-Site Facilitation Date _____

Develop—Relationship
4/5 Working Days Estimated   Start Date _____   Days Actual _____
                               On-Site Facilitation Date _____

Estimated Total: 63 Working Days

Activities After Acquiring "Raw" Research

Input—Competitive Perceptions
1 Working Day Estimated   Start Date _____   Days Actual _____

Input—Importance for Customer Requirements
1 Working Day Estimated   Start Date _____   Days Actual _____

Develop the Measures—Use Fishbone Diagramming, Construct
                        Tree Diagram
5 Working Days Estimated   Start Date _____   Days Actual _____

Complete—Relationship Matrix
5 Working Days Estimated   Start Date _____   Days Actual _____

Calculate—Weighted Importance
3/4 Working Days Estimated   Start Date _____   Days Actual _____

Enter into the matrix—Our Comparison of Our Capabilities and
                        Competitor's Capabilities
2 Working Days Estimated   Start Date _____   Days Actual _____

Finalize—Target Values for the Measures
1 Working Day Estimated   Start Date _____   Days Actual _____

Complete—Correlation Matrix (Optional)
1 Working Day Estimated   Start Date _____   Days Actual _____

Analyze—The House of Quality
1 Working Day Estimated   Start Date _____   Days Actual _____

Estimated Total: 21 Working Days (estimates are based on a 40 × 40
                    matrix).

Phase 3. Strategy Deployment Process— Action Deployment

PHASE 3. (QFD PHASE 2, OPTIONAL)—CHECKLIST

Objective: Identification of key part characteristics, and selection of new or best design concepts.

Action: Technical requirements are translated into part characteristics.

STEP

Transfer—	Priority Measures from HOQ to Action Matrix	1 Day
Complete—	Function Chart "Voice of the Developer"	
Identify—	All Action Attributes—Construct Affinity/ Tree Diagrams	1 Day
Identify—	Degree of Importance of Action Options Rank	1 Day
Transfer—	All "Voice of Company" Requirements from HOQ	1 Day
Complete—	Relationship Matrix	3 Days
Calculate—	Importance Weight of Technical Requirements	1 Day
Analyze—	Action Matrix	1 Day
Identify—	Action Concepts	3 Days
Complete—	Pugh Concept Selection (If Useful)	2 Days
Identify—	Target Values of Parts and Features of Current Product	1 Day
Analyze—	Product Design Matrix	1 Day

Estimated Total: 16 Working Days.

Value Proven First Project Baseline
CIDM Project Support

Executive Visit Day/Preassessment	1 Day
Customer/Mission Day	1 Day
Segmentation Support	1 Day
Market Research and Interview Guide Development	1 Day
Interview Skills Overview and Practice	1 Day
QFD Tools Training	2/3 Days
QFD Facilitation	7/8 Days
Off-site Support	1 Day
Total Estimate	15/17 Days

A detailed outline of activities for each visit:

DAY 1, VISIT 1

QFD Executive Visit (Overview and Team/Project Day)

This working day is designed to present the QFD history, high-level description of CIDM, and executive and company commitments required for success. The Executive Overview takes two to three hours.

Project Preassessment

This tool is used to understand the prerequisites for a successful CIDM/QFD effort. This tool not only reviews the preparation steps but also the readiness of the company managers and marketing research resources to be able to support a customer-integrated development. The tool also defines in more detail the team requirements the company must be prepared to support.

DAY 2/3, VISIT 2

QFD/Customer Mission Day—Segmentation Development

This is an intense working session designed to evaluate and gain agreement among the team on requirements for a successful development effort and to assure the team is prepared to utilize the CIDM/QFD process.

We define and get team agreement on the mission, scope, and objectives. We then work to assure that a complete understanding and agreement exists regarding the market research that is required and acceptable to the team. Out of this part of the "Customer Day," a direction and a responsibility for the market research plan development results. The next part of the day is spent fitting the proper cross-functional team to the task agreed to. The final effort of the day is to do a "rough-cut/high-level" project plan. This will test the effort required and planned for product release and resource commitment expectations. This is an iterative process designed to fit the project, resources, and expectations.

NOTE:

We use both an innovative, simplified, approach as well as very advanced market research. We provide teams and companies with research choices that match cost of effort and timing of efforts with human resource commitments. The range of options has satisfied every one of the hundred-plus projects we have facilitated.

All marketing research approaches conform to "best practice approaches." Single Unit Market Models (advanced choice modeling) are used for segmentation and customer importance setting. We use an advanced method, emerging from the University of Rochester, called "Custoware," to do "text-analyses" if the project timing and value potential warrant it. Segmentation support consists of helping the project team to understand segmentation methods and use the cascade segment visualization process to focus on a segment that is likely to result in profit for the company. This process is iterative in nature and may require additional work beyond this facilitated day to get market data to verify the decisions of the team.

DAY 4/5, VISIT 3

"Interviewing Skills" and "Interview Guide and Survey Development"

We recommend that we provide the team with "Interviewing Skills" and "Interview Guide and Survey Development." These days detail the difference between customer satisfaction/sales visits and "CIDM in-context" data-gathering visits. The team is given support using "voice of value tables" to develop a description of the questions to be targeted in the visit and then given a format for the "Interview Guide." The last part of the day is spent role-playing the visit. This becomes an important learning cycle for new teams about to visit customers.

DAY 6/7, VISIT 4

CIDM/QFD Process Tools and Methodology Training

The next effort is to "train the team" using the QFD tools course, which includes the history of QFD, the reasons for QFD, the QFD process, the use of various market research approaches for QFD, and the QFD matrix.

The training includes "hands-on" exercises designed to allow the team a QFD "house"-building experience.

This process incorporates "tool sets" like the voice of the customer tables (VOCT), and our voice of value table (VOVT) tools. These are designed to help the team decide on the "customer wants" that should be analyzed in the QFD process.

DAY VISIT

CIDM/QFD Facilitationand Ongoing Project Team Support

The approach we follow is just-in-time and in-service team and facilitator training and education. In this regard, we work together to internalize this customer-focused, highly structured and documented, multifunctional team approach. Time and experience have shown that this in-process experiential approach best provides the support required of a first CIDM project and quickly and securely ramps the team's internalization of the process and the company "changes" required.

This approach also supports the secondary objective of developing the required experience and confidence in an internal facilitator.

During the customer day we define and agree on six to eight key points in the project life cycle that require our on-site contact with the team to assure the correct execution of the effort.

QFD/Capture Demo Guide: QFD Management & Documentation Program for Microsoft Windows®

1   Introductory Information

1.1   Copyright

COPYRIGHT by International TecneGroup Incorporated, 1988 –1993. You may freely copy and distribute this Quick Tour Tutorial and the associated demo diskette for evaluation purposes only. You must copy the entire diskette and distribute it in its original form.

1.2   System Requirements

QFD/Capture for Windows can be run on systems meeting the following minimum standards:

- Any system capable of running Microsoft Windows 3.0 or 3.1
- We recommend 386 or 486 processors
- 2MB hard disk required for installation

1.3   Ordering Information

QFD/CAPTURE may be ordered from:

International TechneGroup Incorporated
5303 DuPont Circle
Milford, OH 45150

(800) 783 - 9199   Sales
(513) 567 - 3994   Fax

1.4   Installation

1   **Run Windows.** This demo requires the use of a Windows environment. (NOTE: QFD/CAPTURE is

also available for DOS and Macintosh environments. Please contact us if you need a different version.)

2..   **Insert demo disk into an appropriate drive.** Note whether you used Drive A or Drive B.

3.   **Choose** _File-Run_ **from the Program Manager**

Type A: Setup or B: Setup depending upon the disk drive selected in step 2.

Choose the _OK_ button

4.   **Follow instructions as prompted to complete the installation**

5.   **To start the QFD/CAPTURE demo, Double-Click on the QFD/CAPTURE icon.**

1.5   Demo Limitations

This demo disk of QFD/CAPTURE is designed to let you evaluate our product. With the demo disk, you can use all of the features of the standard software. The only limitations are that you may only build matrices containing 15 or less entries in any list, you may not print the reports, and you may not copy the reports to the clipboard. Everything else is just as you would find it in the standard software.

1.6   Technical Assistance

Should you need any help with this software, please contact us at: (513) 576 - 3993.

2 QFD Overview

2.1 Product, Service, Process or Strategy Development

Any organization developing a product, service, process or strategy needs to answer some basic questions. Among these questions are:

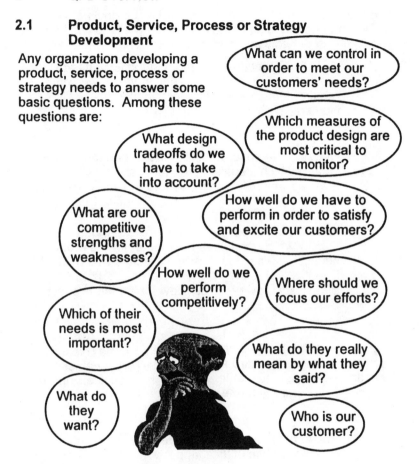

Quality Functional Deployment (QFD) helps ensure that these questions get asked and answered.

2.2   Glossary of Terms

The following terms are frequently used when dealing with QFD. An understanding of their definition will help you be more effective with the software and with QFD. The terms are :

 WHATs - The left-upper room in the Expanded House of Quality, most typically associated with customer requirements; named for identification of what is wanted.

 HOWs - The upper-left list in the Expanded House of Quality which identifies product characteristics or features which can be measured to satisfy the WHATs.

 WHYs - The upper-right list in the Expanded House of Quality which describes the market for the product or service. It also identifies other factors which affect the Prioritization of the WHATs. Named WHYs because they describe why we are developing the Product or Service.

 HOW MUCHes - The left-lower list in the Expanded House of Quality which identifies Target values, products to be benchmarked, and technical importance values for each HOW.

 House of Quality - A term given the QFD planning matrix because of its shape.

2.3   Description of QFD

In the broadest sense, Quality Function Deployment (QFD) is a team-based approach for converting "The Voice of the Customer" into understandable terminology. This is equally important whether you are dealing with a product, a service or a business plan.

The benefits obtained by companies which are successful at QFD include:

◎ Reduced development time due to the early identification and resolution of design problems. This reduces development costs and brings quicker market response time.

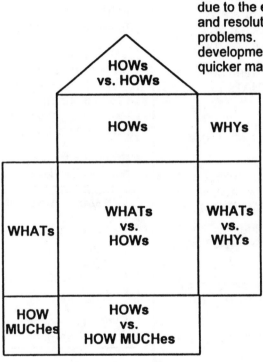

O Improved customer satisfaction with team resources focused on the issues which are important to their customers.

▲ Improved organizational alignment because all product, service or business direction judgments have been agreed to by the team.

2.4   Role of QFD/CAPTURE

QFD/CAPTURE is a software tool designed to support the data management, calculation, analysis, and chart generation needs of teams using QFD, and other matrix methods, for their planning and decision making. In particular, it:

Manages the :

Voice of the Customer (WHATs)

Importance of each criteria (WHATs vs. WHYs)

Design attributes determining customer satisfaction (HOWs)

Relationships between demands and attributes (WHATs vs. HOWs)

Interrelationships between product attributes (HOWs vs. HOWs)

Competitive benchmarking results of product attributes (HOWs vs. HOW MUCHes)

Attribute target values for customer satisfaction (HOWs vs. HOW MUCHes)

Calculates the priority of:
Each want or need

The action for each product attribute

Sorts (to assist in analysis) the :

VOC by related importance or performance data

VOC by related product attributes

Product attributes by related importance or performance data

Product attributes by related VOC items

Creates Charts of the :
Expanded House of Quality

House of Quality (no roof)

Expanded House of Quality Sub-Matrices

QFD/CAPTURE makes QFD practical!

3   **Quick Tour**

Before you familiarize yourself with QFD/CAPTURE, you should realize that it is :

➡ **Optimized to the QFD Process**...Once you realize QFD is not a matrix but a process of gathering, analyzing and making decisions on data, QFD/CAPTURE becomes intuitive.

➡ **Focused on the data, not on the chart**...You need to understand the information contained in the data in order to make the best decisions.

➡ **Very fast**...You will be surprised how fast operations that are either impossible or incredibly time-consuming with other software tools are with QFD/CAPTURE.

➡ **Highly powerful**...It provides you with the data manipulation capabilities necessary to pull information from the data swamp.

➡ **Extremely flexible**...It allows you to do QFD the way you want to.

Let's begin by describing the the syntax used in the demo.

3.1   Demo Syntax :

Pick [xxx]   Double click on [xxx]

Select [xxx]   Click once on [xxx]

Choose [Button]   Click on the named [Button]

[bbb][ccc]   Click on [bbb] menu
                                                        entry. Then click on option
                                                        [ccc]

\<key\>   Press the named key.
"text"   Type text in quotes.

3.2   Exploring On-line Help

Go to **Windows Program Manager**.

Double click on [**QFD/CAPTURE**] . Double click on .

QFD/CAPTURE will initialize and display a representation of the Expanded House of Quality. NOTE : the 'rooms' are 'empty.' This indicates that they contain no data.

Help Index .
This opens QFD/CAPTURE On-line help. You should read "Learning QFD Basics" now. It would also be useful to spend a few minutes browsing and become familiar with Help. It includes a complete example of the different data types stored in the Expanded House of Quality. It also walks you through the definition of calculations and graphs, the most difficult part of using QFD/CAPTURE.

File (Help Window) Exit .
The on-line help screen will close.

3.3 Opening a Matrix, Looking in the Rooms

File Open .

Choose 'Lunch' . Open .
Opens the Lunch database. NOTE : the 'rooms' are now filled in indicating that they contain data.

Rooms WHYs .
Enter the WHYs room. Conceptually, this list describes the current market. It tells WHY this product needs to exist. Includes customer groups your product must satisfy, their relative importance, and lists of competitive products. NOTE : see WHYs Command in on -line Help for complete example.

Select ' Parents.' <Enter>
Selects Parents entry and allows editing of information. This Dialog Box (also available through choosing Edit More about Entry shows specifics of a WHY. In this case, the type of Parents entry is Number; the column will contain numeric data, formatted as Integers (whole numbers). The Parents' input is weighted by the .7 multiplier. NOTE : there are many other parameters that can be changed.
<Esc>
Closes Edit Entry Dialog Box.

Select ' Improvement Factor' . <Enter>
Opens Edit Entry Dialog Box for Improvement Factor. NOTE : this entry contains Calculation data. The calculations are defined in the More button.

Choose [More][Calculations][Percent Change] .
A calculation is usually defined using a calculation-specific dialog box. Notice the wide variety of calculations supported by QFD/CAPTURE. In this case, the Percent Change calculation requires 3 parameters : percent of scale covered by one interval (.2), number of the entry containing ratings of current perceived performance (6), and number of the entry containing future perceived performance (9). The entry numbers identify WHY entries.

<Esc>
Closes Calculation Dialog Box.
<Esc>
Closes Edit Entry Dialog Box.

Select ['Bar'] <Enter> .
Selects Bar entry. (NOTE: you may need to scroll down the entry list to find Bar.) Allows you to view the Edit Entry Dialog Box. Note that the type of this entry is Graph. The graphs are defined through the [More]button.

Choose [More][Graph][Bar] .
A graph is defined using a dialog box. QFD/ CAPTURE supports both line and bar graphs. In this case, the bar graph requires that the user enter the number of the entry to be plotted, the color for the bars and the type of scaling desired.

<Esc>
Closes the Bar Graph Dialog Box.
<Esc>
Closes the Edit Entry Dialog Box.

Choose [File][Exit List] .
Exits the WHYs room. When you leave the WHYs list, the Window containing the list is closed. NOTE : you should now be looking only at the Main Screen.

Choose [Rooms][WHATs] .
Open the WHATs room. This lists the customer's wants or what is to be achieved. When the "House of Quality" is used with end user requirements, WHATs are customer statements about desired product benefits. NOTE : you will find a complete example under WHATs Command in on-line help. Add new entries at the list's end or use the [Edit][Insert]command to insert new entries elsewhere in

the list. Experiment with the Level Menu commands, which organize your lists into groups or categories.

Rooms (QFD/CAPTURE Main Window) **WHATs vs. WHYs** . Opens the WHATs vs. WHYs room, while leaving the WHATs room open. This relationship matrix prioritizes the WHATs based upon marketing information. Usually, the data contained in this matrix are importance ratings from customer groups' perceptions of each of the WHATs. Expected WHATs ratings of competitive products' performances can also be included here. Averaging the ratings and determining where your product is perceived relative to your competition establishes each WHAT's overall importance. NOTE : see WHATs vs. WHYs Command in the on-line help. Since the WHATs and WHATs vs. WHYs rooms are open, you can jump back and forth quickly between the two. These rooms are really just different views of the data; a change made in one room is automatically updated in all the other rooms.

<Right Arrow> <Down Arrow> <Left Arrow> <Down Arrow> Scrolls through the WHATs and the WHYs lists. The relationship ratings appear in the "Value" box (center). Change some of the values, if you wish, by typing in a new value. Repeat the process until you feel comfortable.

File (WHATs vs. WHYs Relationships) **Exit Relationships** . Exits the WHATs vs. WHYs room.

File (WHATs List) **Exit List** . Exits the WHATs list. NOTE : again, the Main Screen should be the only visible window.

Select **HOWs** (in the Expanded House of Quality outline). Enter the HOWs room. NOTE : clicking within the outlines of the rooms of the Expanded House of Quality is equivalent to using the Rooms Menu. By measuring and controlling the HOWs you ensure satisfaction of the customer's requirements. Typically, HOWs are measurable, controllable, design parameters for which target values may be established. Sometimes, HOWs are also called Quality Characteristics. NOTE : the HOWs Command of on-line help shows a complete example.

File (HOWs list) **Exit List** . Exits the HOWs room.

Rooms (QFD/CAPTURE Main Window) **WHATs vs. HOWs** .
Opens the WHATs vs. HOWs room. This relationship
matrix correlates what a customer wants from a product
and how you can meet those standards. *It is the core
matrix of QFD.* Relationships here are usually defined
as strong, medium, weak or no relation. NOTE : see
WHATs vs. HOWs Command of on-line help for a
complete example.

Select **'Easy to Make'** .
Selects the entry from the WHATs list.

<Right Arrow> <Down Arrow> <Down Arrow> .
Scrolls through each list. Note how **'Easy to Make'** is
related to each HOW by reading the relationship value in
the box in the middle of the window. Change the values
of a few relationships by choosing or typing in the desired
value. Repeat until you are comfortable.

Choose **Relationship Note** .
Allows entry of background information in the Relationship
Note box. There is no limit on the length of a note, and
notes can be attached to all entries and relationships in
the Expanded House of Quality.

<Esc>
Closes the Edit Relationship Dialog box.

File (WHATs vs. HOWs) **Exit Relationships** .
Exits the WHATs vs. HOWs room.

Rooms (QFD/CAPTURE Main Window) **HOW MUCHes** .
Opens the HOW MUCHes room. This list gives a
technical description of the marketplace. It includes
entries for capturing the priority and target for each of the
HOWs. NOTE : the HOW MUCHes Command in on-line
help contains a full example.

Double click **'Ideal Lunch'** entry.
Opens Edit Entry Dialog box. NOTE : the height of the
row accommodates approximately 20 characters in a cell.

<Esc>
Closes the Edit Entry Dialog Box.

File (HOW MUCHes) **Exit List** .
Exits the HOW MUCHes room.

Rooms (QFD/CAPTURE Main Window) HOWs vs. HOWs .
Enters the HOWs vs. HOWs room, the matrix that forms
the roof of the "House of Quality," and thus gives it its
name. It identifies interactions between HOWs.
Relationships are rated from Strong Positive to Strong
Negative or None. Two HOWs that help each other meet
target values are rated Positive or Strong Positive.
Negative or Strong Negative means reaching one HOW's
target value complicates another HOW's target realization.
NOTE : see HOWs vs. HOWs Command in on-line help.

File (HOWs vs. HOWs) Exit Relationships .
Exits the HOWs vs. HOWs room.

Rooms (QFD/CAPTURE Main) HOWs vs. HOW MUCHes .
Opens the HOWs vs. HOW MUCHes room. This
relationship matrix helps you decide the plan of action.
Typically, it includes calculated values identifying the
importance of each of the HOWs. The information
establishes realistic target values so you meet customer
requirements. NOTE : see HOWs vs. HOW MUCHes
Command in on-line help.

<Right Arrow> <End> <Left Arrow> <Down Arrow> .
Scrolls through the target values for the HOWs and HOW
MUCHes. Repeat until you are comfortable.

*NOTE : If you had added new data throughout this process,
the House of Quality would now be complete.*

Sort (HOWs vs. HOW MUCHes) By Right . **SELECT** all HOWs.
Sorts data by relationship strength. NOTE : to select the
HOWs, press the left mouse button and slide the cursor
down the HOWs list (on the left). The HOWs should now
be in reverse video.

Select 'Importance of HOW Execute Leave Sorted Ok .
Displays items in priority order to assist in analysis.
NOTE : the HOWs and WHATs list can be sorted by any
set of related values.

File (HOWs vs. HOW MUCHes) Exit Relationships .
Exits the HOWs vs. HOW MUCHes room.

Rooms (QFD/CAPTURE Main) Reports .
Enters the Report Preview room. Verify that you have the
expected data defined and calculated.

<Page Down> <Page Down> <Right Arrow> <Ctrl+End> .
Scrolls through the full size view of the Expanded House of Quality.

⌐Formats¬ (Reports Preview) ⌐Zoom¬ .
Zooms out to view the entire matrix. You can jump to a particular location in the matrix quickly and verify that all pertinent data is present. Use the arrow keys to move the zoom box around the screen.

⌐File¬ (Reports Preview) ⌐**Print Report**⌐**Scale to Page**⌐**Ok**¬ .
Prints the current report on an attached printer, with the output scaled to fit on one page. NOTE : the demo package will NOT actually print. Printed Matrices throughout this book were generated by QFD/CAPTURE.

⌐Formats¬ (Reports Preview) ⌐**WHATs vs. WHYs**¬ .
Displays another report available on QFD/CAPTURE.

⌐Options¬ (Reports Preview) .
Pulls down the Options Menu. Experiment with the options for customizing reports, defining relationships, and naming rooms. NOTE : QFD/CAPTURE can also handle Pugh Concept Selection.

⌐File¬ (Reports Preview) ⌐**Exit Reports**¬ .
Exits the Reports Preview room.

⌐File¬ (QFD/CAPTURE Main) ⌐**Save As**¬ "Lunch2" <Enter> .
Saves the database under a new name, leaving the original demo database intact. The Main Window caption should now read Lunch2. From this point on,⌐**File**⌐**Save**¬ will save changes to the new database.

⌐**Utilities**⌐**Transform**¬ .
Enters the transform utility. This allows the user to transform data from the HOWs and HOW MUCHes rooms into the WHATs and WHYs rooms of a new database. The data is copied with all relationships intact. This function supports the multiple phases common to QFD.

Select All **HOWs** .
Select all the HOWs by pressing the left mouse button and sliding the cursor down the list of HOWs. All of the HOWs should now be in reverse video.

Select $\boxed{\text{'Importance of the HOWs'}}$ <Ctrl> $\boxed{\text{'Ideal Lunch'}}$.
Selects Importance of the HOWs and Ideal Lunch from
the list of HOW MUCHes. NOTE : select the former and
press the left mouse button. Hold the **<Control>** key,
drag the cursor to the second option, and pick with the
mouse. The two entries should be in reverse video.

Choose $\boxed{\text{Execute}}$.
Execute the transformations, copying the selected HOWs
and HOW MUCHes and their relationships to the new
database.

Type "Tran1" . <Enter> .
Names the new database. The database can now be
opened using the $\boxed{\text{File}}\boxed{\text{Open}}$ command in Main.

Choose $\boxed{\text{Done}}$.
Closes the transform utility.

$\boxed{\text{Utilities}}\boxed{\text{Extract}}$.
Allows you to create a new database containing a subset
of the current database. You can experiment with the
utility although it will not be explained in depth at this time.

NOTE : QFD/CAPTURE also includes utilities to export and
import data from a text file and to append two databases.

Choose $\boxed{\text{Done}}$.
Closes the Extract utility window.

$\boxed{\text{File}}\boxed{\text{Exit}}$.

This exits the Quick Tour of QFD/CAPTURE.

*Spend some time exploring the software! Its power and
flexibility provide you with the tools to implement powerful
QFD applications!*

4 Building a Matrix

Having finished the QFD/CAPTURE Quick Tour, you should try
to build a matrix from scratch. The matrix in this section is
similar to the one contained in on-line help; however, this one
will be built in layers. You will start with a very simple QFD
matrix and add layers of additional information to demonstrate
how QFD can be used to answer additional questions.

4.1 The World's Simplest QFD Matrix

This matrix will answer the following questions :

> ✓What do they (our customers) want?
> ✓Which of their needs is most important?
> ✓What can we control in order to meet our customers' needs?
> ✓Which measures of the product design are most critical to monitor?
> ✓How well do we have to perform in order to satisfy and excite our customers?

NOTE : see page 255 for a more complete list of QFD questions.

Double click .

> Clears out the data that is currently in the software.

4.2 What Do the Customers Want?

Rooms WHATs .

Enter the data at the top of the next page :

"Easy to make sterile" <Enter>
"Stays placed correctly in mouth" <Enter>
"Tells me when failing" <Enter>
"Tells me when temperature is dangerous" <Enter>
"Does not break when dropped" <Enter>
"Usable by all ages" <Enter>
"Cost effective" <Enter>

> These are the customer demands for this matrix.

The question has been answered and documented.

File (WHATs Window) Exit List .

4.3 Which Requirement is Most Important?

Rooms WHYs .

Type **"Importance to Healthcare Professionals"**. **<Enter>**

> Establishes the type of customer and creates a column to capture the importance values they give to the WHATs.

Click twice on 'Importance to Healthcare Professionals .

> Opens the dialog box that allows you to set the properties associated with that entry.

(Under **Data Format**)Choose ⟨Real⟩ ⟨Ok⟩ .
 Changes the format of the numbers associated with this
 entry.

⟨File⟩ (WHYs Window) ⟨Exit List⟩ .
 Closes the WHYs room.

⟨Rooms⟩⟨WHATs vs. WHYs⟩ .

Type the following data

4.9 <Enter> <Down Arrow>

4.1 <Enter> <Down Arrow>

3.2 <Enter> <Down Arrow>

1.9 <Enter> <Down Arrow>

2.8 <Enter> <Down Arrow>

3.1 <Enter> <Down Arrow>

1.3 <Enter>
 Enters the customers' importance values.

⟨File⟩ (WHATs vs. WHYs Window)⟨Exit Relationships⟩.
 Closes WHATs vs. WHYs room.

*The question is answered and the relative importance of each
of your customer's requirements has been documented.*

4.4   What Parameters Can Be Controlled?

⟨Rooms⟩⟨HOWs⟩.

Type the following requirements :

"Time to sterilize at home" <Enter>
"Conformance of shape to mouth" <Enter>
"Number of internal performance checks" <Enter>
"Out of normal T range warning method" <Enter>
"FMEA rating of design" <Enter>
"Designed age range" <Enter>
"Cost/usage" <Enter>

These measurable, controllable design parameters are
used by your cross-functional team to describe how you
can satisfy your customer's requirements.

The question has been answered and documented.

File Exit List .
 Closes the HOWs window.

4.5 Which Measurement is Most Important?

Rooms WHATs vs. HOWs .
Enter these relationship strengths. The WHATs are listed on the left, the HOWs on the right, and the strength to be chosen in the middle.

Easy to make sterile	(9)strong	Time to sterilize at home
	(3)moderate	Conformance of shape to mouth
Stays placed correctly in mouth	(9)strong	Conformance of shape to mouth
	(3)moderate	Designed age range
Tells me when failing	(9)strong	Number of internal its performance checks
	(3)moderate	FMEA rating of design
Tells me when temperature is dangerous	(9)strong	Out of normal T range warning method
	(3)moderate	Designed age range
Does not break when dropped	(1)weak	Time to sterilize at home
	(1)weak	Conformance of shape to mouth
	(1)weak	Number of internal performance checks
	(9)strong	FMEA rating of design
Usable by all ages	(3)moderate	Conformance of shape to mouth
	(1)weak	Out of normal T range warning method
	(9)strong	Designed age range
Cost effective	(1)weak	Time to sterilize at home
	(1)weak	FMEA rating of design
	(9)strong	Cost/usage

This defines the HOWs' predictions of a WHAT's success. Calculating the weighted sum of these relationships on a column-by-column basis prioritizes the list of HOWs.

File (WHATs vs. HOWs Window) Exit Relationships .

Rooms HOW MUCHes .

Type **"Importance of Design Parameters"**. **<Enter>**

Click twice on **'Importance of Design Parameters'** .
Opens the dialog box associated with the entry.

(Under **Type**)Choose **Calculation** .
Marks type of data associated with the entry as a
calculation.

(Under **Data Format**)Choose **Real** **More** .
Displays the Calculation Dialog box.

Calculations **Absolute Importance** .
Requires identification of which column of the WHYs
contains the data giving the importance of the WHATs.

Type **1 <Enter>** . **Ok** .

*When the calculations are updated, you will be able to identify
which design parameter is most important.*

File (HOW MUCHes Window) **Exit List** .

4.6   How Well Do We Have to Perform?

Rooms **HOW MUCHes** .

At end of list, type **"Target Values"**. **<Enter>**

Double Click **'Target Values'** .
Opens dialog box. Allows you to set the properties
associated with that entry.

(Under **Type**)Choose **Text** **Height** Type **"20"** **OK**
Indicates that this row of the matrix will contain text data
and that approximately 20 characters should be visible.

File (HOW MUCHes Window) **Exit List**

Rooms **HOWs vs. HOW MUCHes**

Select **'Target Values'** from right hand list.

Select **"Time to sterilize at home"**
Type the following :
"1/2 min maximum" <Enter> <Down Arrow>
"Flat tip with holder" <Enter> <Down Arrow>
"Battery and circuitry" <Enter> <Down Arrow>

"None" <Enter> <Down Arrow>
"25 Minimum" <Enter> <Down Arrow>
"2+ Years" <Enter> <Down Arrow>
$2.20 Maximum" <Enter>

The question has been answered and documented.

| File | (HOWs vs. HOW MUCHes Window) | Save As |

Type **"Thermo". <Enter>**
    Saves data in Thermo database.

| File | Exit |

You have now completed building the world's simplest matrix.
Exit the software, if you wish. However, if you have more time,
please continue to experiment.

Notes

Chapter 1

1. The four-phase model of QFD was developed by a Japanese reliability engineer named Makabe. In the United States, the QFD training courses offered by the American Supplier Institute (ASI), a training and consulting firm based in Dearborn, Michigan, are built around the four-phase model. Other models of QFD exist; some of the better-known ones are briefly described in part II.

2. The phrase "constancy of purpose" is from W. Edwards Deming; it is one of his fourteen points of quality management.

Chapter 2

1. "Hard" data is quantitative or qualitative data that come from direct measurement or observation. "Soft" data include things like opinion or "educated guesses," e.g., the assumed or postulated strength of a relationship between an engineering characteristic measure and a customer need.

2. Throughout this book, the word "product" may be understood to mean "strategy, product, or service."

3. The "PiGiSH" mnemonic was created by Barry Weiss, a QFD facilitator at Hewlett-Packard Company.

Chapter 5

1. Sherry Bosserman and Jeanne Stoner, "QFD Introduction to Motorola—A Study in Change Management," *Transactions from the Sixth Symposium on Quality Function Deployment*, 1994.

Chapter 8

1. David Bohm, *On Dialogue*, available from Pegasus Communications of Cambridge, Massachusetts. This pamphlet was edited from a transcription of a meeting that took place on November 6, 1989, in Ojai, California, following a seminar given by Professor Bohm. It is highly recommended reading. The late Dr. Bohm was a fellow of the Royal Society and emeritus professor of theoretical physics, University of London.

2. Chris Argyris, *Harvard Business Review*, July–August 1994, pp. 77–85, and his book *Overcoming Organizational Defenses*, Allyn and Bacon, 1990.

3. First learned and adapted from a similar pledge used by Dr. Mike Munn of the Gaia Center for Quality.

Chapter 9

1. Michael E. Porter, *Competitive Advantage*, Free Press, New York, NY, 1954.

2. Elemer Magaziner, Project Linguistics International, Inc, Sedona, Arizona. A developer of an understanding that customers have many viewpoints, also a lecturer and author regarding organizational learning.

Chapter 10

1. C. Douglas Ballon, AIA, "Ultratec Tijuana," *The Sixth Symposium on Quality Function Deployment*, 1994, pp. 63–80.

2. CustoWare is a trademark of Polansky, Incorporated, 3159 South Winton Road, Suite 203, Rochester, NY 14623.

Chapter 11

1. Stuart Pugh, "Concept Selection—A Method That Works," *Proceedings, ICED*, Rome, 1981, pp. 497–506.

Chapter 13

1. Yoji Akao, *Quality Function Deployment*, Productivity Press, 1990.

Glossary

ADAPTIVE LEADERSHIP

An emerging management approach that the authors have named based on the directions of the business environment. This capability focuses on being able to proactively understand the market effects on the organization, through the use of CIDM, and then make "value delivery" changes in-process rather than sequential decision-making approaches that are characterized by slow change.

AFFINITY DIAGRAMMING

A team process to arrange customer "needs" statements into natural groups. This is a data reduction process.

Ah-ha

A discovery made by a team practicing CIDM; recorded on TeamTalk chart.

ANALOG CHANGE

This "change" management experience implies a systematic planned and continuous change over time. This approach provides a mindshift rather than simply a tool set introduction. But it requires organizational patience to achieve—demanding a long-range expectation for change rather than a short-term results expectation.

BIG P

This euphemism defines the sum of all actions a company takes to supply a market solution. The term includes all the marketing, engineering, manufacturing, sales, delivery, and service actions when viewed as a whole by the customer.

CASCADE SEGMENTATION

A method to determine and visualize targeted market segments.

CATCHBALL

In achievement of targets, the process of "give and take" between levels of management to agree on the way to hit targets.

CHOICE DECISION-MAKING

This describes the actions to understand how the customers will make decisions to buy a solution, not what they will consider satisfaction. This understanding allows the company to better define attributes in its solution that will predict a purchase for the specific segment they have targeted. In the dimensions of quality aspects, this approach is supported by efforts to understand the "structure" (meaning, in detail, of the words of the customers) of the attributes they ask for.

CLOSED-END SURVEYS

This term describes a survey that asks very specific questions, usually that have predefined answers as choices. In relation to in-context marketing research questions, which are very "open" or broad, these questions lend themselves to understanding satisfaction issues for known attributes but do not support the discovery of "hidden" customer needs and wants, or potential delight attributes.

COMMUNICATION PLAN

The actions and responsibilities to assure ongoing methods of sharing understanding and learning among team members and other stakeholders.

CONCEPT SELECTION MATRIX

A matrix that allows for relative comparison and selection of viable solution choices based upon customer-prioritized measures, functions, or other decision criteria.

CONSENSUS

A state of agreement among team members in which all may not agree fully with issue at hand, but all agree to support the decision of the team.

CONTEXT

The words and phrases surrounding a customer's statement of need that adds meaning to the real need.

CONTINUOUS IMPROVEMENT

The process of forever creating better quality; a mind-set for never accepting the current quality; necessary especially in competitive markets because customers' perceptions are always changing.

CONTROLLED EXPERIMENTS

These market research systems will assess the potential appeal of various approaches to solving customer problems. They are able to test a range of selling strategies, such as advertising themes, new or current product concepts, and price levels. This tool is used after market identification and idea generation during the idea test phase of the solution realization effort. They tend to be very accurate, and with regard to cost, very valuable.

CROSS-FUNCTIONAL

A type of working environment in which appropriate representation is available for the task at hand; having all needed organizational functions represented early in the development process.

CUSTOMER DIMENSION MATRIX

A tool used by a CIDM team to identify the full customer definition for the segment they are in process of understanding. It is used to target the "customers" they need to contact during the understanding phase. This tool leads the team to identify the customers they must contact because they are the ones they sell to and/or are influencers of the customer they sell to. The team must understand who the customers are to be able to adequately define a solution. The Customer Dimension Matrix was influenced strongly by the work of Elemer Magaziner.

EXPECTATIONS LADDER

This is a tool used in CIDM to plot the different attributes of the "target values" that are established by the team to describe customer-defined (expected) targets for the "measures" the customers use to know that the company solution meets their expectations. This is a visual graphing of these variables designed to allow the team to reach agreement and record the various decisions made.

FUTURE QUALITY

This describes the efforts of a company to utilize "choice" based and "in-context research" processes in making decisions on strategy and solution. The effort then is to engineer in the quality using a multifunctional team and "customer voice" data rather than technology driven efforts. Historical quality is measured after the product is released using satisfaction studies. Future Quality is measured before the product is designed using "choice" based studies.

HIGH-ENERGY ADAPTIVE TEAMS

This term is used to define an organizational unit more advanced than a team. Of the three types of organizational units—work group, team, and more than a team—HEATs will action decisions more on their own, provide bidirectional empowerment, and be more successful than the other types. CIDM will allow these teams to become more effective and more adaptive through its structure, and customer-focused interaction.

HISTORICAL QUALITY

These are the activities to support functional quality assurance; they are those activities that provide the defined quality. It is usually measured by satisfaction studies—aimed at getting the customers' reaction to "how well and consistently we are able to deliver the solution." This is traditionally where total quality control has been focused.

JOIN-UP

In the team-building process, reaching a good, open working relationship among team members; in interviewing, reaching a comfortable conversation level with the customer during check-in.

LITTLE P

This term defines the actual product. The implication is whatever the customer sees as the primary solution, without any marketing, sales, manufacturing, delivery effort, is the *Little p*. The personal computer, the car, the liquid in the can, etc.

MANAGEMENT PRODUCT

Originally defined by Bill Barnard to describe management's responsibility and reason for using CIDM/QFD to develop strategy, this approach defines the output of a management team as a product—and the responsibility of managers to include in their direction some early understanding of the segments to focus on and early understandings of the customers' decision-making process as defined by their "choice decision-making criteria." It defines a structured process with defined actions and in-context customer contact in assuring strategy and action definition.

QUALITY CHARACTERISTICS (MEASURES)

These describe the point at which the CIDM/QFD team will begin the translation from the understanding they have of the wants and needs of the customer to a description of the "characteristics"—value, strategy, product, part, process, etc., that the customer will use to understand or know that the company is providing what the target segment wants, needs, and any potential "delighters." Various terms are used to describe these, such as "hows," "substitute quality characteristics," "characteristics."

SOLUTION REALIZATION PROCESS

Defines a more complete process for understanding, defining, developing, producing, and supporting "products" for the market. In the "value" world describes the comprehensive set of actions that a company will need to accomplish to provide benefit. The CIDM/QFD approach is more conducive to providing this solution than traditional "product development" processes.

STRATEGY DEPLOYMENT

A process used in CIDM/QFD to assure that strategy and action decisions are accomplished. This process was influenced by the Hoshin Kanri methodology used in companies like Hewlett-Packard, Boeing, and Pierce and Stevens and developed by Japan. This is a practical application of Hoshin's principles.

SUSTAINABLE COMPETITIVE ADVANTAGE

This results from our solution development activities using CIDM. It is the expectation we have from the efforts to identify the most profitable segments to do business, understand the customers' business problems in context, understand the "choice" as well as the "satisfaction" levels of the customer, and make decisions within a cross-functional team viewpoint. The fact that we do this from a "value delivery" viewpoint is also part of the reason that we will expect that our "differentiation" potential will allow us to have a competitive advantage in our solution development.

TEAMTALK

This is an approach developed by Rick Norman that includes the tasks of acknowledging and archiving the issues, actions, and Ah-ha's that the team uncovers during the CIDM process. These data comprise the "outputs" of the project and this structured data capture and reporting process assures the recognition of the full value of the CIDM process.

TECHNOLOGY ADOPTION MECHANISM

Describes a model that includes a varied tendency to accept or "adopt" new technologies at a different pace among members of a population of potential users of new technologies. For purposes of this book we describe the population as a bell-shaped curve, those that are innovators as well as those that are laggards, the mean population falling into the early and late majority classification.

VALUE DELIVERY PROPOSITION

This output of the solution realization process is the total "promise" that the company can deliver to the customer. It is made up of the "story" the company tells about its value to the customer. This "promise" is designed to define the differentiating reason that causes a customer to desire the solution the company can deliver. It is the sum of all of the BIG P components.

VOICE OF VALUE TABLE

A tool used by the CIDM/QFD team to understand the areas of "choice" importance the customer has, especially those areas that are not being provided in the marketplace today. It includes a $100 test of customer choice importance and a $1,000 test of the customers' perception of suppliers' performance in the market place.

Suggested Reading

Akao, Yoji. *Quality Function Deployment: Integrating Customer Requirements into Product Design,* Productivity Press, Cambridge, Massachusetts, 1990.

Barnard, Bill. *Corporate Strategy and Linkage to P&IC Tools,* Manufacturing Principles and Practices Seminar Proceedings, American Production and Inventory Control Seminar, Las Vegas, Nevada, May 1990. (One of the first papers describing the use of QFD to set and link corporate strategy and production decisions.)

————. *Quality Methods in Identifying Manufacturing Strategy and Linking P&IM Tools,* 33rd International Conference Proceedings, New Orleans, Louisiana, October 1990. (A follow-up paper on the use of QFD to define production actions by understanding the customer and linking to these decisions.)

————. *Using Quality Function Deployment to Align,* Transactions from the Fourth Symposium on Quality Function Deployment, Novi, Michigan, June 1992.

————. *QFD-Empowering the Multi Disciplined Team for Manufacturing Excellence,* 35th International Conference Proceedings, Montreal, Canada, November 1992.

————. *Using Quality Function Deployment to Align Business Strategies and Business Processes with the Customer,* GOAL/QPC 9th Annual Conference, Boston, Massachusetts, November 1992.

————. *The Innovation Edge: Creating Strategic Manufacturing Breakthroughs Using the "Voice of the Customer"* and *Strategy Deployment* (details the integrated use of Hoshin Kanri to assure action on customer-integrated decisions), American Production and Inventory Control Society, Atlantic Coast Symposium, Greensboro, North Carolina, February 1994.

Barnard, Bill and Bill Kern. *Building the NII,* NTU Satellite Network—Advanced Technology & Management Programs Broadcast July 1994. (Discussion on processes to be used in building the National Information Infrastructure. This broadcast detailed a linked customer data acquisition and customer-integrated project management process.)

Barnard, William (Bill), and Thomas F. Wallace. *The Innovation Edge: Creating Strategic Breakthroughs Using the Voice of the Customer,* Oliver Wight Publications (omneq), Essex Junction, Vermont, 1994.

Brassard, Michael. *The Memory Jogger Plus: Featuring the Seven Management and Planning Tools,* GOAL/QPC, Methuen, Massachusetts, 1989.

Clausing, Don, and Stuart Pugh. "Enhanced Quality Function Deployment," *Design and Productivity International Conference,* Honolulu, Hawaii, 1991.

Daetz, Douglas. "QFD: A Method for Guaranteeing Communication of the Customer Voice Through the Whole Product Development Cycle," *Conference Record of the International Conference on Communications,* vol. 3, Boston, Massachusetts, June 11–14, 1989, pp. 1,329–1,333.

———. "Planning for Customer Satisfaction with Quality Function Deployment," *Proceedings of 8th Inter-national Conference of the Israel Society for Quality Control—Jerusalem,* November 1990.

De Vera, Dennis, Tom Glennon, Andrew A. Kenny, Mohammad A.H. Khan, and Mike Mayer. "An Automotive Case Study," *Quality Progress,* vol. XXI, no. 6 (June 1988), pp. 35–38.

Griffin, Abbie, and John Hauser. "The Voice of the Customer," *MIT Marketing Center Working Paper* #91-2, January 1991.

Dobyns, Lloyd, and Clare Crawford-Mason. *Quality or Else: The Revolution in World Business,* Houghton Mifflin Company, Boston, 1991.

Imai, Masaaki. *Kaizen: The Key to Japan's Competitive Success,* Random House, New York, New York, 1986.

Juran, J. M. *Juran on Planning for Quality,* Free Press, New York, New York, 1988. (Chapters 2 to 7 relate directly to steps involved in creating the initial QFD matrix, although the term "quality function deployment" is not used in the book.)

King, Robert. *Better Designs in Half the Time,* GOAL/QPC, Methuen, Massachusetts, 1987.

Kogure, Masao, and Yoji Akao. "Quality Function Deployment and Company-wide Quality Control in Japan," *Quality Progress,* vol. XVI, no. 10 (October 1983), pp. 25–29.

Liner, Marilyn, Douglas Daetz, Frederic Laurentine, and Rick Norman. "A Road Map for Gathering Data from Customers: Lessons from Experience," *Transactions from the 6th Annual Symposium on Quality Function Deployment,* Novi, Michigan, June, 1994.

McQuarrie, Edward F. *Customer Visits: Building a Better Market Focus,* Sage Publications, New York, New York, 1993.

Mizuno, Shigeru, ed. *Management for Quality Improvement: The Seven New QC Tools,* Productivity Press, Cambridge, Massachusetts, 1988. Originally published in Japanese by JUSE Press, Tokyo, 1979.

Mizuno, Shigeru, and Yoji Akao, eds. *QFD: The Customer-Driven Approach to Quality Planning and Deployment,* Asian Productivity Organization, Tokyo, Japan, 1994.

Magaziner, Elemer. "What Has Happened to the Voice of the Customer?," *Journal of the Quality Assurance Institute,* January 1993.

———. "Finding a Future," *Executive Excellence,* June 1993.

Newman, Richard G. "QFD Involves Buyers/Suppliers," *Purchasing World,* vol. 54, no. 10 (October 1988), pp. 91–93.

Norman, Rick. "QFD: A Tool for Concurrent Product/Process Development," NEQCCC, 1990.

———. "QFD: The Practical Implementation," National Electronics Packaging Conference, 1992.

———. "Tailoring QFD to Your Needs," 1992 Symposium on QFD, Novi, Michigan.

———. *QFD: What's It All About? Where's It Headed?,* National Electronics Packaging Conference, 1994.

Norman, Rick and Alan Leeds. "Integrating Voices of Customers to Drive Organizational Learning," GOAL/QPC's Tenth Annual Conference, 1993, Boston, Massachusetts.

Norman, Rick, Robert Hales, and Dilworth Lyman. "Concurrent Product/ Process Development, A Concurrent Design Methodology: Making It Happen," Society of Manufacturing Engineers, 1990.

Norman, Rick, Johann Lindig, and Alan Leeds. "Aligning a Concurrent Product Development Process Using Momentum QFD: A Case Study in

Letting the Voice of the Customer Drive the Conceptualization of a New Leak Detector," 1993 Symposium on QFD, Novi, Michigan.

Porter, Michael E. *Competitive Advantage,* Free Press, New York, New York, 1984.

Richmond, Peterson, and Charyk. *Introduction to Systems Thinking and ithink™,* High Performance Systems, 1992.

Ross, Phillip J. "The Role of Taguchi Methods and Design of Experiments in QFD," *Quality Progress,* vol. XXI, no. 6 (June 1988), pp. 41–47.

Saaty, Thomas L. *Decision Making for Leaders,* University of Pittsburgh, Pittsburgh, Pennsylvania, 1988.

Scholtes, Peter R. *The Team Handbook,* Joiner Associates, Madison, Wisconsin, 1988.

Senge, Peter M. *The Fifth Discipline: The Art and Practice of the Learning Organization,* Doubleday/Currency, New York, New York, 1990.

Shaikh, Khushroobanu, and F. Timothy Fuller. "Does Success Have a Secret? Can Quality Function Deployment (QFD) Help You Design Better Products and Services?," December 1987. (Available from K. Shaikh, an HP employee.)

Shillito, M. Larry. *Advanced QFD: Linking Technology to Market and Company Needs,* John Wiley and Sons, New York, New York, 1994.

Shillito, M. Larry and David J. De Marle, *Value Its Measurement, Design & Management,* John Wiley and Sons, New York, New York, 1992.

Smith, Preston G., and Donald G. Reinertsen. *Developing Products in Half the Time,* Van Nostrand Reinhold, New York, New York, 1991.

Thackeray, Ray J., and George Van Treeck. "Quality Function Deployment for Embedded Systems and Software Product Development," paper presented at GOAL/QPC Sixth Annual Conference, Boston, Massachusetts, December 5, 1989.

Transactions from a Symposium on Quality Function Deployment, Symposia 1-6, 1989–1994 (in June each year), Novi, Michigan. (Available from the American Supplier Institute, Dearborn, Michigan, or GOAL/QPC, Methuen, Massachusetts.)

Wheatley, Margaret J. *Leadership and the New Science: Learning About Organization from an Orderly Universe,* Berrett-Koehler Publishers, San Francisco, California, 1992.

Wyckoff, Joyce. *Mindmapping—Your Personal Guide to Exploring Creativity and Problem Solving,* Berkley Books, New York, New York, 1991.

Zultner, Richard E. "Software Quality Function Deployment: Applying QFD to Software," *Proceedings of the 13th Rocky Mountain Quality Conference,* June 1989.

Index

About the Authors

Douglas Daetz, Quality Maturity System Operations Manager, Corporate Quality, Hewlett-Packard Company (Palo Alto, California), developed the training and support infrastructure for HP's QFD initiative from 1988 to 1991. For the past three years, Doug has supported the expansion and revision of HP's internal assessment and improvement program, the Quality Maturity System (QMS), and is himself a QMS lead reviewer. He earned a B.E. in electrical engineering from Yale and a Ph.D. in electrical engineering and computer science from the University of California at Berkeley. Before joining HP, Doug was the director of quality at Shugart Corporation and an assistant professor of industrial engineering at Stanford University. He has authored articles on design for manufacturability and QFD, and he invented the multivariable display technique now called the radar chart or spider diagram.

William (Bill) Barnard is a practitioner in Customer-Integrated Decision-Making, supporting small- to medium-size companies across the world in their move from technology-driven to customer-"balanced" strategy, product, and process developers. Bill utilized the experience he gained while working at Hewlett-Packard (Major Account Project Manager and Senior QFD Facilitator) and ATT/NCR (Director of QFD Processes) to develop an integrated methodology he calls "Customer-Integrated Decision-Making" (CIDM).

He was one of the first to use QFD for strategic planning and in-context customer visits. He has successfully supported teams in electronics, consumer goods, consulting services, software, and network management. He is one of the first to successfully integrate QFD with "Hoshin Kanri" (an action deployment process)—a technique he calls "strategy deployment."

Bill has responsibility experience in manufacturing operations management, industrial planning, automation control systems, information processing systems development, and strategy and product development.

Bill has facilitated over one hundred projects in the internalization of CIDM/QFD, including having rollout responsibility in two large companies. He works worldwide today with a client list that includes Hewlett-Packard, Motorola, Pierce and Stevens (a Pratt and Lambert Company), Senco (a Sencorp Company), Scotsman, Franklin Industries, Modicon/AEG, Hermann Miller, and European-based organizations.

Bill provides support for advanced customer data acquisition processes that involves customer "choice-based" satisfaction understanding and has business associated relationships with companies providing these services.

He has a degree in computer science, is certified by the American Production and Inventory Control Society (CPIM), is a Senior Fellow at the Center for Competitive Change at the University of Dayton and External Faculty to Motorola University. Bill was a member of the APICS Certification Council, a member of the Material Requirements Planning (MRP) exam committee for twelve years, and a founding member of the Systems and Technology (S&T) certification exam committee for three years.

Rick Norman, a practitioner of QFD since 1987, is an experienced student of the product development process. He has fifteen years' industry experience in engineering, design, and marketing roles for aerospace, consumer products, medical instruments, and consulting firms. Founder and leader of the San Francisco Bay Area Users Group, his current focus is creating collaborative environments for organizations to practice structured planning and decision-making by adapting the principles of systems thinking and CIDM. He holds a bachelor of science degree from the United States Military Academy at West Point and served five years in the U.S. Army Corps of Engineers before joining industry. He is a certified QFD instructor for GOAL/QPC, Methuen, Massachusetts, and a member of the Learning Organization Network in Santa Clara, California.